Image for Investigation:

About my Father

Christoph Meckel

VP Festschrift Series:

Volume 1: Christine Brooke-Rose
Volume 2: Gilbert Adair
Volume 3: The Syllabus
Volume 4: Rikki Ducornet
(Edited by G.N. Forester and M.J. Nicholls)

Reprint Titles:

The Languages of Love
The Sycamore Tree
The Dear Deceit
The Middlemen
Go When You See the Green Man Walking
Next
Xorandor/Verbivore
by Christine Brooke-Rose

Three Novels — Rosalyn Drexler
Knut — Tom Mallin
Erowina — Tom Mallin
The Greater Infortune/The Connecting Door — Rayner Heppenstall
The Penelope Shuttle Omnibus — Penelope Shuttle
Conversations with Critics — Nicolas Tredell
The Utopian — Michael Westlake

New fiction:

Mirrors on which dust has fallen — Jeff Bursey

other Verbivoracious titles @

www.verbivoraciouspress.org

Image for Investigation:

About my Father

Christoph Meckel

Translated by Dr. Stan Jones

Verbivoracious Press

Glentrees, 13 Mt Sinai Lane, Singapore

This edition published in Great Britain & Singapore

by Verbivoracious Press

www.verbivoraciouspress.org

ISBN: 978-981-09-6762-8

Printed and bound in Great Britain & Singapore

First published in Germany as *Suchbild. Uber meinen Vater* by Classen
Verlag, 1980.

First published in Great Britain by Hutton Press Ltd., 1987.

Acknowledgements

The translator would like to thank Christoph Meckel for his willingness to answer questions on his text.

The publisher would like to thank Dr. Stan Jones for his enthusiasm in revising the original translation.

Introduction

BEN WINCH

To write about someone means: destroying the reality of his life in favour of the reality of words. (p.41)

Christoph Meckel—I grow surer—is a naive/childlike genius. Let me qualify that; I don't want to condescend. He's "beginner's mind" genius. Yogi genius. He keeps things *fresh*. About the man himself I know next to nothing—what I could learn in English on the internet. And of course there's that rule about three points to make a straight line. But on the basis of *Image for Investigation* (a memoir) and *The Figure on the Boundary Line* (short stories and a novella), so disparate in tone and subject yet so much his own, I know, if nothing else, he's *himself.*

What links *Image* and *Boundary Line*? Precision. Vigilant invention. ("Of course there are many who can invent and cast their spells without a second thought," he writes in *Boundary Line*: "But with me, nothing ever comes of boredom.") Honed craft—the craft of the whittler, the condenser. Craft that's dense and light at once; packed with allusion yet free of dead weight; nimble, poised, able to pin a butterfly to a tree, yet able to bring down the tree with explosive force if necessary. Christoph Meckel, if you like, is a miniaturist—like Antonio Tabucchi (a friend, according to Tabucchi) yet more earthy, more raw. He's *direct*, he pierces through, he cuts to the core.

And make no mistake, this book *cuts*. The surgeon's metaphor, oft-used, is accurate, since Meckel attempts nothing less than a dissection, an autopsy in search of a root-cause. Luckily or not, the corpse is bloated; he has much to work with. Meckel's father was poet, reviewer, journalist, obsessive diarist. "Dependably and pedantically," writes Meckel, "he archived it all."

> I had not intended to spend time on my father. It did not seem necessary to write about him. His case, a private one, was closed. [...] Since I read his war diaries, I cannot let his case rest any longer; it is no longer private. I found the notes of a person I did not know. (p.31)

Image For Investigation, then, is an act of *need*, personal and political: the attempt, by the son of a former German officer in the Second World War, to account not just for his father's actions but for the actions of a generation. Note I said "account for", not absolve, not condemn, though Meckel's language is unsparing, torn from a heart shut tight and wounded by love. *Image for Investigation: About My Father* (in German, *Suchbild. Über Meinen Vater*; in French, *Portrait Robot Mon Pére*), as its English title can't suggest, is an identikit portrait of a spirit at large—an essential soldier (officer-class), a man (though he be pitied) to be feared. Not a war criminal as Hollywood would have it, maybe, but the unthinking servant of a criminal state, who never repented nor assimilated the fact of his guilt.

Writers from Tadeusz Borowski to Danilo Kiš tell us in one way or another of the worst a human can be or experience, of the darkness (always inferred, though Borowski comes close to naming it) in our hearts. What Christoph Meckel (a child among the rubble—born, like Kiš, in 1935) does is more subtle. Rather than monsters and victims, Meckel gives us an ordinary bourgeois, a pawn. But for all his strong words he *feels* for his subject, and doesn't deny it. Nor does he seek to make excuses, to win us over, to make of his father an anti-hero, or anything so glamorous or larger than life. Meckel's father was a scared man, a hurt man, finally a broken man. His caste of spirit, his inborn arrogance, his blithe self-absorption—Meckel nails them all. The father's tragedy is his soul's wounded terminal immaturity. But to *nurture* that soul, to rescue it, is what Meckel proposes. As the Buddha said: "Only love dispels hate," after all.

Of course at times it all but turns the stomach, but not through its depiction (virtually non-existent) of gore. This is not the prison camp depravity of Borowski, but a domestic, drawing room depravity: the naive arrogance of a sheltered second-rate poet given to yearning for "action and manly adventures" when literary dinners get too slow; who believes himself "heir and DESCENDENT of the German Spirit" (the capitals are Meckel's, as if to mimic the "nationalistic clichés" whose "vapours" dope his protagonist); who is "carried into the barracks in the sedan chair of a master race", though of course he's just "CANNON FODDER" like them all. And whereas Borowski's protagonist has no illusions, Meckel's takes his to his grave, resists "the proper definition of his self" and dies believing (or professing to believe) his every act of cowardice courageous, his every betrayal a sacrifice for the greater good.

> He never again came so close to knowing himself. [...]
> There he confronted—INWARDLY MOVED—the insight
> that there was such a thing as German guilt. [...] But
> personal guilt—NO. He had wanted what was worthy and
> had done his best. (p.45)

So though Meckel "would like to tell tall tales for his benefit", for the most part he can do no more than watch as the story unfolds, all the while weighing the influence on his own life, wounded in turn. ("He stood like a black cloud between the child and the world.") Nonetheless, by the story's end, in an inspired act of creative courage, he liberates his father's child-soul.

> Can you dilute the water?
> Child's play.
> Can you eat the darkness?
> You know I can. (p.95)

Which goes to show, Christoph Meckel isn't naive at all, only determined to not lose sight of the childlike, in this book of all books, with his father's child-shade looking on. If *The Figure on the Boundary Line* was like Hans Arp "taking a line for a walk" ("The highest purpose," said John Cage, "is to have no purpose at all") then *Image for Investigation: About My Father*, while its route is still governed by the "divining-rod", digs a line deep in the sand, a moral boundary. Meckel's compassion, his dexterity with the knife, his lack of sentiment when sentiment would only slow his hand, his seeing *around* his subject, his willingness (an artist's) to explore—these traits make *Image* an uncommon work of biography, a hybrid which, in places, is hardly biography at all. Perhaps the older Meckel's true achievement was his child's "unnerving education at the hands of language", for which we thank him, even as we mourn.

A second volume of memoir concerning Meckel's mother exists but is not yet translated into English. I trust it and other works will eventually appear in our language.

Translator's Note

STAN JONES

In 1969, Christoph Meckel published a "Gedicht für meinen Vater" (Poem for my Father, *Frankfurter Allgemeine Zeitung*, 15 June, 1969). Its first verse anticipates the image of his father he develops in *Suchbild*:

Lebenslang
lebendig begraben
in einem grauen Grab Melancholie,
dort wirst du nicht verlangt, und bist allein
eingerichtet mit zerbrochenen Glocken,
Sonnenblumen, Laub und nächtlichem Wind
dort geht du umher, einen kleinen verklingenden
Donner hauchend in eine Flasche Wein
Und hältst ein Lachen
Vor dein zersprungenes Gesicht.

(Lifelong buried alive in a grey grave of melancholia; you're not sought after there and are installed all alone with broken bells, sunflowers, leaves and the night wind; you go around there huffing a little fading thunder into a bottle of wine and holding a smile up in front of your fractured face).

"Image for Investigation" is the nearest I could get to Meckel's title for his book. It connotes an image both inviting investigation and reflecting that process, and the notion of a "Suchbild" also refers to the pictures posted publicly in Germany of loved ones people were seeking after the war.

Meckel's book is a form of biography, which shades into autobiography —all biographies must do—as its author traces his own reactions to what he remembers of his father (although he did warn me against seeing it as an autobiography when we discussed *Suchbild* in October 1985). As such, it belongs to a sub-genre of 20th century German literature, the father-biographies written by children who grew into adulthood in Germany in the post war years. Important examples are: Ruth Rehmann's *Der Mann auf der Kanzel* (The Man in the Pulpit, 1987), Siegfried Gauch's *Vaterspuren* (Traces of my Father, 1979), Brigitte Schwaiger's *Lange Abwesenheit* (Long Absence, 1980), Paul Kersten's *Der alltägliche Tod meines Vaters* (The everyday Death of my Father, 1978) and Peter Härtling's *Nachgetragene Liebe* (Belated Love, 1980). Few have been translated into English.

Suchbild tends to censure Meckel's father rather than reconciling with him, although Meckel does say he does not want to be "in the right" over his topic and would gladly have made things up and created fantasies for his father's benefit. In a wider context, he reflected on his own profession and his generation's baleful heritage when received the "Bremer Literaturpreis" for his book in 1981: " . . . when proposals and the lack of them balance each other out, jargon goes round in circles like a faulty record and anger and despair are lying bled white on the floor—then a moment of total calm arises. In this moment poetry begins." (translation by SJ) He sees the literary creativity of the individual as illustrating how the despair over having to own a seemingly hopeless historical situation might be overcome. His attitude can, of course, be dismissed as an idealizing rehabilitation of himself and his profession to ensure its continued relevance in the modern world, a relevance only recognised by those of us who keep faith with literature, anyway.

As one such believer, I hope my translation of *Suchbild* does allow the significance, and value, of Christoph Meckel's writing to emerge, fraught though its subject matter may be.

IMAGE FOR INVESTIGATION:

ABOUT MY FATHER

I

I am keeping the happiness of the first memory.

Next to my father in the DKW,[1] very likely too small to look out of the window; fast driving on the Schöneicher Chaussee beyond Friedrichshagen, to the east of Berlin. The car roof open, a bright day, I leaned my head back and looked up into the sky where the leaves fluttered and closed over me, a giddy whirl of shadow and light—whilst my father steered the car; this memory over and over again, sunlit and gloomy highroads, driving at night, Brandenburg Province, dead straight highroads and fast driving, a feeling of security and blind trust, a wonderful certainty with him there.

*

He administrated the days of his life dependably and pedantically: all the experience of living onto the files. He archived it all.

He collected and conserved with discrimination. Organised, stacked, bundled, deposited and preserved. Remembered, inspected, cleaned and kept together.

A web-spinning zeal related the facts of his biography together and found in them a reason for constantly asking what had been seven years ago and what in turn would be seven years hence. Today's headache and Adalbert Stifter's[2] birthday; this evening's glass of wine and a drinking session in Blansingen ten years ago. In this way, just as tangible as it was irrational, the past was inserted as backing under each day in the calendar; dead time was woven into living time. His nose for things past was infallible. A melancholy revitalisation.

He collected newspaper clippings, family photos, bills and carbon copies of all kinds. He collated the letters from his family, from his friends and acquaintances, congratulatory notes, thank-you letters, circulars and obscure printed matter. He went beyond what was necessary for organising his records and collected articles he had written and other people's reviews as they related to his topics. He hoarded bits of wood, stones and tram tickets, collected the first or last maple leaves of the year and left them behind, complete with a record of date and place, as bookmarks. He collected pictures by the painters of his home-landscape (Bizer, Scherer, Dinkelsbühler), invitations to concerts, posters and genealogical tables, as well as documents of all sorts about grandsires, aunts, cousins and distant relatives. He noted down the dates of friends' deaths, of their weddings, birthdays and name days;[3] he noted their accidents, lucky breaks, illnesses and telephone calls. He recorded the cause of death for all the people he knew about by hearsay and the deaths of film actors whom he had admired thirty years before.

Drawers full of yellowed paper packages. He noted down dreams, meetings with acquaintances, the casual and the CONSUMMATED CONVERSATIONS, the results of tennis matches, shooting practice and blood tests. He noted down full moons and shooting stars, collected locks of his children's hair, recorded how many glasses of wine he had drunk and the day's weather: high pressure, low pressure and bodily reactions, rain and Föhn wind and his corresponding mood. Catalogues of the weather, snows-of-yesteryear collected from four decades. Menus, flyers, plane tickets, hotel bills and cinema programmes. He collected badly typed marching orders, programmes from mess evenings during the war and proposals from the Divisional Command in Poland for celebrations honouring Hitler. He collected photos of landscapes and architecture and every detail on the history of his home-province: family annals, poets and grand dukes, maps, monuments and Goethe's[4] nieces.

Life savings in a paper piggybank. He was constantly reorganising it and destroyed very little. Doggedly, he committed his final illness to the archive, depressions, bouts of fever and attacks of pain, prescriptions, drugs and treatments, the effects and side-effects of cortisone, the names of his doctors and nurses, the remnants of his hope (in a stumbling hand) and the view from the sick-room onto a spring day.

*

The world of my father is the landscape of Baden between Karlsruhe and Basle. It extends along the southern edge of the Black Forest up the Rhine to Waldshut, Schaffhausen and Constance, from there in a northerly direction to Donauschingen, Tuttlingen, Rottweil and Balingen, via Heckigen and Horb to Freudenstadt, further on to Baden-Baden and Karlsruhe, then up the Rhine again to Straßburg, straight across Alsace to Colmar, Mulhouse and Belfort, to the Belfort Gap and the foothills of the Jura. It embraces the southern and northern Black Forest, the high plateau of Baar towards Swabia, eastern Alsace and northern Switzerland, the upper Rhine, the Kaiserstuhl, the eastern slopes of the Vosges and the Breisgau basin. It is the landscape of Johann Peter Hebel[5] together with all the Swabian, Helvetian and French variants of the Alemannic language. It lies in the centre of European history, was captured by Sweden, and moulded by French and Austrian culture. In all of its regions, the landscape is beautiful; it ranks amongst the most beautiful in Central Europe: varied, lush, idyllic and fertile, open to the South, West and North and governed by strong contrasts in climate. The stupendous irruption from the South in summer; the onrush of the Föhn[6] in a February night. Stupendous too the masses of snow and the burdens of leaves. A land of rivers, gardens, vineyards and the Mittelgebirge.[7] Crops, cattle raising, and growing industrialisation, lime-works, cement-works, glass-works, breweries and all sorts of woodworking are there. Health resorts, winter sports centres, spas and international tourism in all seasons are there. Potatoes, asparagus, rapeseed and maize, corn, barley and sunflowers are there. Storks, trout, cows, pheasants, wild pigs, bees and a few wild turkeys. Smoked ham, must and homemade bread are there. Innumerable orchards and kitchen gardens are there and thus, apples, cider-apples, pears, plums, peaches and nuts. Asters, lupins, mallows and woodbine are there. June turns red with roses, cherries and poppies. Wood and resin, lime honey and pine honey too, nettles, nightshade, thistles and honeysuckle, ferns and mosses in unusual forms are there. Raspberries, blackberries, bilberries and blueberries, the edible and the poisonous mushrooms, lime trees, beeches and birches, larches and rowan trees. The pines of the high Black Forest and the poplars along the old channels of the Rhine are there. Polluted rivers and clean streams, nature reserves with very rare birds, plants and orchids. Above all, wine is there. The Markgräfler and the Kaiserstuhl wines are there, the late Burgundies and the "ice wine"[8] are there. Countless rare vintages are there, and wine from barrels in country pubs is there. The Chasselas from small cooperages and the headache-wine mixed for export by the big vintner syndicates are there. Catholicism and local dialect poetry from beyond the forests and beyond belief are there. Superstition, carillons on the town halls and the Christian Christmas are there. The arrogance of the provincial mule-head, with ideas like THE SOIL and ROOTEDNESS, is there, together with a chronic, largely ignorant and almost benevolent but also hard-headed, rustic chauvinism directed against lowland Germans, Frenchmen, Burmese, children, students, protest singers, Swiss, Icelanders, Jews, spaghetti-eaters, Chileans, negroes, Russians and interlopers (the chauvinism remains within bounds as long as the above-named do not set foot on local soil). The broad-arsed, self-righteous consciousness of one's home ground, with male-voice choirs, women's choirs, children's choirs, mixed choirs, bands in local costume and brass bands, is there. Fire brigades, local-history societies, tables for regulars only and the forenoon glass in all its forms are there. A few hundred Hebel museums, with Hebel pictures, Hebel aphorisms and senior schoolmasters honorarily officiating and Hebeling away, are there. The reactionary mentality of land-holding, ownership and heritage, of respectability and order, is there. The Badische Zeitung, the Schwarzwälder Boten and any number of newspapers with every editorial stance between pinkishly socialist, deep black conservative and a trusty colourlessness are there. High schools, universities, botanical gardens, town libraries and institutes of viticulture, night-schools, technical schools and tree nurseries, publishers, theatres, museums, important trading companies and the archbishop are there. Congresses of all the parties take place, and that trusty, sought-after lifestyle, Black Forest cuisine with piles of chops in a cosy parlour, is there. Clinics for alcoholics, old-people's homes, prisons, slum-clearances, juvenile crime, satellite towns, unemployment and all the century's unsolved problems are there. Cheap cottage industry is still there and produces souvenirs and straw shoes. The rented hunting ground with all the trimmings, the weekend cottages of the rich people from Switzerland are there. And, in spite of everything, the first successful citizens' protest against the building of a nuclear power station is there. Nothing, apart from the sea, is lacking here, and everything on offer is abundant.

*

In the middle of the province stands Freiburg capital of the Black Forest, state capital of Southern Baden, a thousand years old, a mid-sized city, charming, situated on the old salt road between East and West, at the crossroads between Vienna-Paris and Frankfurt-Zürich; the birthplace of my father and the place of his death, the beginning and end of what he knew about the world. Here stands the Freiburg Minster, the most beautiful structure in Christendom, a wonder of the world from Western culture, the only cathedral completed in the Middle Ages, with horn-blowing angels, organs, gargoyles and tracery spires curving gently outwards. An air raid destroyed the town; the Minster remained standing. Since the town was rebuilt, it has been in danger. Air pollution is eroding the stonework; the red sandstone is soft and flakes off. The restoration of the Minster, the replacing of its stonework, has been under way for decades and never ends. Its structure will never again be seen without scaffolding.

My father loved the bells of the Minster (on clear days you can hear them up into the mountains). On New Year's Eve, he stood at the window and listened to the bells; he listened to them on all the feast days, could distinguish between their tones and knew their names: little silver, SUSANNA DARKMOUTH. He needed the bells: stupefaction by the thunder on the wind, consciousness lapsing amidst tolling and airborne concerts. He wanted his last resting place up above the bells, in the winds of the upper Rhine, in the Octagon.[9] The Minster was the centre of the ALEMMANIC HOMESICKNESS, the furthest reach of all his wishes and fits of melancholy, the embodiment of his atmospheric Catholicism and, from childhood on, a symbol of solace. He sought and needed solace, craved it; he took refuge in consolation and dreamed his dreams there. In place of just about everything he lacked (and today I think that he lacked almost everything), he adopted obscuration. There were too many things, any of which could seem comforting to him; a faith in one's destiny and in the order of the world; trivial elements from a bourgeois religiosity had come down to his generation. They swaddled him in his youth and held him fast his whole life long. Solace was the nebulous talisman of this faith and the need for it a weak point in his nature. He needed the consolations of sentiment more than perceptivity, dialectics, critical insight . . . He clung to straws of reassurance, sought painfully to experience yearning and hankered after an ecstatic intensification of his sensitivity (organs, organs, organs resounding and Chopin). He sought solace, compensation via solace, an exemplary solace to reconcile all opposites (and he found it too—in TRANSCIENCE). He became the apostle of solace, with no followers. His yearning for solace isolated him, alienated people of enlightened mind and did not enjoy any understanding in his family. Needing solace—perhaps the result of an irrational and fundamental capitulation—was murky warmth and repulsed me. He found the solace necessary for living in ideas of family, nature and art; he found it above all in his landscape. That meant the Black Forest with the timbered farmyards, the ravines, the slopes, the meadows and the high woods, the scent of leaves rotting, barked trunks, the silhouette of Mt. Belchen in the sun and the snow. That meant the villages out there in the summer, the Kaiserstuhl and the orchards by Kirchhofen. Old wells and chapels, research in a monastery library, that all consoled him. The customs and legends of the landscape, the graveyards, the walls around manor house parks and the inn-signs consoled him. The oft-repeated walks to Sölden, Horben or St Ulrich consoled him. The graves of his relatives, the graves of poets and Hebel's letters, the homely metre of the poet Pfeffel,[10] all consoled him. A summer evening in Opfingen consoled him and enriched his life. He drove to the villages and walked across country and, as far as that brought him solace, he was soothed and approachable as a person. The knowledge of South German art-history, an almost erotic affinity for wood and stone, his pleasure in observing and relating his observations made him unbeatable on his good days; dissipating his knowledge made him carefree. Altars, madonnas and peasant art took on life through him and his explanations. He travelled to Amsterdam and Florence, and undertook so-called BAROQUE JOURNEYS through the South German autumn, viewed absolutely everything that was worth seeing and came back to his daily round a fulfilled person.

*

Picturesque figures from the family. Lawyers, professors and generals, peculiar grandmothers and black sheep. Sporting ties and moustaches, the notables with the church's blessing, a pension and a spouse. One had brought Prussia to Japan and created the Emperor's army; another had whipped his children at the dinner table. Some uncle or other painted the hunt in Bavaria, and there was someone descended from Goethe's mother.

They bowed out when the talk turned to my grandfather. The talk in the family had him down as a monster . . . It pictured him as a saturnine gentleman who had devoured his own children. The children were not to his taste and he spat them out. My father was a spat-out child.

The grandfather was considered a significant architect (his father had trained as a mason and architect in the Minster workshop). He had developed a sort of concrete which proved itself unusually durable (it withstood the bombs of the Second World War). Oxblood-red paint for facades was his invention. He had restored the Römer[11] in Frankfurt, built office blocks, churches and bridges, and all that in a moderately historicising style, a mixture of the practical, the gothic and the baroque. The master cultivated a severe image, an iron mask, domineering and anti-German (he hated the Third Reich unreservedly): a respected boss and a man feared by everyone. He seldom laughed, at the most briefly and sharply; he loved his own dignity and his dog. In the background, his wife figured as an honest, female being, who was locked into the household and lived her life, supervising and comforting, at a standstill. My father was the youngest child. He found his first solace in her closeness. The restricted, female being (she was a happy hedonist) blossomed in old age into a merry widow. She spent her fortune on sweets. I knew her as a woman in black, at once harmless and tyrannical, a fat family creature with a hatpin, hairnet and arthritic fingers, which dispensed sweets to the tram drivers in Freiburg.

The misanthropist broke the spirit of his children. No one escaped his scorn, except as a victim of some misfortune. My father suffered under a chronic lack of affection and stuttered at an early age. Whatever he did to win his father over met with terse and cold scorn. He sought his regard all his life, without any response. The gentleman was impeccably dressed, with spats, a walking stick and a dog on a lead. He broadcast iciness and orderliness and beat his sons in the cellar. For him nuts were shelled and plums peeled. The maxim governing his children's education ran: you are nothing, you are capable of nothing, do your homework. It resurfaced word for word from my father when he read my first poems.

He froze in the shadow of this frosty gentleman. He fled into a lifelong yearning for landscape. He had his father to thank for his humble, almost servile attachment to family and childhood, their figures and locations. He had him to thank for his addiction to his home territory and for an insurmountable fear of life. He had him to thank for his sense of principle and punishment and his absolute belief in authority. His childhood was a hole from which he crept, beaten.

Without his wanting or wishing it, and in a weaker form, he imitated his father's nature.

On the surface, his youth seemed quite normal. Born in 1907, two older siblings, middle-class family, well-off, respectable existence. Holidays in Black Forest villages and in Switzerland. The change from gas to electric lighting, the first Zeppelin[12] and the first tram. The First World War, for the provinces something exotic, with a few bombs, soldiers and parades. His father was stationed in Alsace; on a journey to see him, he saw destruction for the first time: a gutted house, a wrecked vehicle. Admiration and fear; the war was something unhallowed. A youthful love affair, high school, a summer by the sea, then boarding school in a country town in Baden. Catholic and nationalistic schooling. Successes on football fields and walks on lonely paths. Youthful scrapes, juvenile escapades. Sensitivity to nature. Tendency to melancholy, to the idyllic and to musing. Early heart-trouble and frequent illness. Reading of poetry in the summerhouse.

The youth of a talented young man in the provinces.

*

Freiburg, a beautiful town in all seasons. Of a morning, ham and wine in the GRAPEVINE. The Minster Market and the Black Forest flower-girls warming themselves at braziers on winter mornings. The mountains of apples and cartloads of potatoes, the smell of fruit in the mist, the clicketing nuts. Gurgling, splashing, echoing springs, soundless streams at the roadside and soughing trees. The leaf-strewn steps on the Castle Hill, the plane trees in the graveyard, the flaming fox-red autumn in the Colombi Park. The Mozart masses in the Minster, the litanies, metallic twitterings from the organs, their growling and whistling. Sixteen-voiced tolling of the Minster bells, a swaying resonance in the Föhn, in the west wind, in the snow.

II

He came to Berlin in 1929, married in 1931 and lived with his wife in various apartments, a few years on the Laubenheimer Platz, a quarter inhabited by literary bohemians, with Peter Huchel and Martin Kessel as neighbours (Tucholsky had lived there for a while too). Peter Huchel, Günter Eich, Martin Raschke and Horst Lange[1] were his friends. They took my father's DKW (Günter Eich and he were the first writers of their generation to own cars) on long weekends into the Brandenburg March. They strolled along lakeshores and talked about poetry, climbed into fenced-off parks and peered into the mansions through binoculars. They met in pubs on the Alexanderplatz, along with wives and friends. His private life seemed to be pretty carefree; he was young and unsuspecting and had much to hope for. They went to Weimar and viewed the Goethe house, visited Martin Raschke in Dresden and took trips together to Saxony and Zinnwald. A trip with Günter Eich through the autumn in Franconia was particularly beautiful. He knew Elizabeth Langgässer well, had seen Becher, Brecht and Benn[2] from a distance and was earning money from Berlin Radio with plays, book reviews and scenarios adapted from various classics. They visited Huchel in rural Miechendorf, gave parties and showed off the first of the children. He spent a few summer weeks in Günter Eich's holiday house on the Baltic several times. Huchel, Eich and my father in the dunes at Prerow. The oat-grass found its way into their poetry, the rain, the stars, and whatever they felt was timeless. They worked together, played table tennis, and read each other their new poems in the evenings.

In 1937 my father built a house. He bought a cheap site in the east of

Berlin and was proud of putting up a house to his own design in a short time and for not much money. It stood at the edge of the Schöneiche woods, was white, with red and white painted shutters and a pointed gable (the ARYAN ARCHITECTURE as prescribed in the Third Reich); it was surrounded by a garden, grass and trees and across the road was the edge of the wood with birches and firs, and beyond that the eastern plains stretching down to the Oder, flat and endless under towering skies, with tilled fields, marlpits and old highroads (the Prussian cobbles were still intact). A path edged with sunflowers led up to the house, and there was a sandpit for the child. There was an arbour for sunny days. It all looked peaceful, charming and permanent. Next door, Tucholsky's[3] wife was kept hidden, but they only found out about that after the war.

I often asked my father what the Thirties meant for him, and how he lived, and above all: what he and his friends thought of the times, and never got a particularly enlightening response. Whilst Brecht, Döblin and Heinrich Mann emigrated, Loerke and Barlach were smothered to death in Germany, whilst Dix and Schlemmer[4] went to earth in South German villages, whilst musicians, scientists and filmmakers disappeared, whilst colleagues were defamed, persecuted, banned, books burned and pictures confiscated, he wrote tranquil verses in a traditional style and built a house in which he wanted to grow old. He scarcely seemed to notice the exodus of the Jews, the Communists and the intellectuals, the sudden or gradual disappearance of the whole avant-garde. Whilst the SA[5] marched, the Reichstag[6] burned, he himself was witness to deportations (a squad interrogated him too and searched through his books), he carried on writing stories and poems in which the times did not figure. He was not alone in this attitude. All sorts of literati from his generation (a whole phalanx from the youngest among the intelligentsia) went on living amazingly removed from their times. They encapsulated themselves in nature-poems, slipped away into the seasons, into things eternal, ever-valid, timeless, into the beauties of nature and of art, into the notion of solace and into the belief that temporal miseries would pass. He was ambitious, athletic, healthy and inexperienced, and he had a name to make for himself. Günter Eich had studied Sinology in Paris, and Huchel had travelled for years throughout Europe, but he had only lived in Germany and had known nothing but the German mentality. He did not, not in any thought or deed, leave the orbit of a brassbound, idealistic, German-literary existence as a bourgeois. There was no thought of flight or of shifting to another country. It is not likely that there was any talk of emigration between him and his friends. That did not seem necessary. They could live, had families and houses, were hardly called into question over their profession, nor were they because of their backgrounds or their views. They had just started their work, had settled into their first, modest success, into a literary, professional and personal self-confidence; outside of Germany, they had no chance, were too young anyway and did not possess names that could have secured them an existence in other languages. My father lived in the Third Reich without any bother, lived blindly on into an ever-shortening future, stressed his repugnance, contempt and pride and trusted impotently in the power of the spirit. Everything beyond that he left to fate. FATE—the notion could be had for nothing and had been whispered to him in his cradle. In the Thirties, the ideology of German Idealism drifted around the place, obtrusive, sombre and inescapable, was polished up by the State's propaganda, concealed radically different philosophies and could be converted—according to personal need—into amazingly thick blinkers. Like Martin Raschke he was by no means insensitive to the ATMOSPHERE of National-Socialist progress, but he was, and remained, incapable of recognising the reality of its politics. I LIVE FOR THE MOMENT. I LIVE FOR THE DAY. Nature poetry set itself up in an arbour, but the arbour stood on a ground of iron and was surrounded by walls of barbed wire

In the mid-Thirties, Huchel, Eich and my father went on a car trip to Wiepersdorf. There, on the lower edges of the Fläming plateau, at the edge of the March village, stands the ancestral home of the Arnim family. Achim von Arnim and Bettina Brentano[7] had lived there a hundred years before; their graves lie in the grounds, a beautiful setting for German Romanticism, with stables, an orangery and an overgrown park. It was a bright, timeless day in summer. Each of the three undertook to write a poem with the title WIEPERSDORF and with their day together as its subject. My father's poem no longer exists; the poems of Eich and Huchel became famous: DEM LEBEN, WIE SIE'S LITTEN, /AUF'S GRAB DER BLUME LOHN:/ FÜR ACHIM MARGERITEN / UND FÜR BETTINA MOHN! (To life as they endured it, on their graves flowers in recompense: for Achim marigolds, for Bettina poppies!). And Huchel fashioned a poem about autumn out of that day, with the magnificent opening: WIE DU NUN GEHST IM SPÄTEN REGEN, / DER MOND UND HIMMEL KALTER FLOSST / UND AUF DEN LAUBVERSCHWEMMTEN WEGEN / DEN RISS IN DIE GESPINSTE STÖSST—(as you walk now in the late rain that bears moon and sky in a colder flow and thrusts the rift into the webs on the leaf-washed paths).[8]

*

From 1929 to 1932 Martin Raschke published three volumes of a monthly periodical called DIE KOLONNE ("Journal of the Dresden Young Writers' Group"). It was the only forum for the most recent generation and looked above all to Berlin. It contained poems, prose, criticism and discussions on the state of literature. Huchel, Lange and Eich published in it and my father had his first poems printed there. DIE KOLONNE became the launching point for the sort of verse that came to define NATURE POETRY in the Third Reich and afterwards. When the journal ceased, the poets remained friends. DIE KOLONNE, and still more the friendship between its various authors, created the beginnings of something like the atmosphere of inner emigration. In private conversations, dissent found a voice, a retreat out of the times into poetry.

The young poets hailed from the provinces, brought their landscapes to Berlin and established them in literature. Günter Eich came from the Oder and Horst Lange from Silesia. Huchel brought the Brandenburg March, Raschke the Harz Mountains and my father the Black Forest. All of them brought closeness to the earth and the seasons, existing, finding refuge, and breathing in unison with nature. Most of them shared the same unprogrammatic and poetically intuitive tendency: away from the age and its civilisation, away from politics and psychology. Love poems involved DREAMS and VISIONS, but not much eroticism and no sexuality at all. The sciences and technology did not figure. Community and society did not exist. Together with Raschke, Eich wrote the MONATSBILDER DER KÖNIGSWÜSTERHÄUSER LANDBOTEN (THE MONTHLY BULLETINS OF THE KÖNIGSWÜSTERHAUSEN COURIER) for the radio.

Bert Brecht was for Eich the creator of BAAL[9] and Gottfried Benn a distant fascination. In landscape motifs and in the tranquillity of their language there lay concealed an anarchy which romanticised nature (with my father it was probably the hankering after peace and quiet). That signified a new trend, coming after the close of the Expressionist era, after working-class writing and cosmic poetry, after cosmopolitan and asphalt literature (Goebbels had contributed the term ASPHALT-POETS and then declared them fair game for persecution). The trend conformed to the deepened inwardness of the Thirties and was predestined for BLOOD AND SOIL.[10] My father and Raschke sited their provinces on nationalistic soil; Eich, Huchel and Lange remained aloof. Huchel was reckoned, as he wanted to be, a pure poet. An elemental force in the lyric sphere, precocious, uninterested in theory or thesis, a phlegmatic phenomenon, reticent, an amiably melancholic Bohemian with the experience of a richly varied life in France behind him. He came from the rural proletariat, had grown up among day-labourers, tinkers and tenant farmers, farmhands and milkmaids, and his sure sense of justice made him immune to any jargon. He saw and heard the TWELVE NIGHTS[11] coming. In the KOLONNE and among the group of friends, he was the only one who knew anything about Marxism (a sleepy gleam in his left eye). Eich expressed the most trenchant scepticism over the times. This apparently indifferent man, reserved, hesitant, a PETIT-BOURGEOIS CHINESE, made the most obvious withdrawal into himself. "Responsibility towards the times? Not the least bit. Only towards myself." And: "One can say of the rain that it promotes the growth of plants, but it would not occur to anyone to maintain that that is what it intends. The greatness of lyric poetry and of all art is, however, that they, although created by human beings, are as purposeless as natural phenomena." He rejected the involvement of the State in art (and any response from a poet to questions of politics), as well as any ideological demands. There was, as he wrote, no place for timebound and propagandistic language in poetry. But there was no talk of FATE either. "What is the essence of an era? Certainly not its external appearances, the aeroplane and the dynamo, but the change wrought upon humanity by it. Yet who among us knows where the change is taking us; who can see today the thoughts and objects in which our times express themselves most clearly? If you demand that lyric poetry should commit itself to its times, then the most you require is that it should commit itself to Marxism or to anthroposophy or to psychoanalysis, because we don't know which of these systems of thought and of living will be the universal representative of our times, we only know that each tendency and each movement claims that role for itself."

A problematical self-isolation of the lyrical ego. It led Eich and Huchel to write less and less and, in the end, not to publish any more lyric poetry. One removed oneself, among friends, private and passive, and seemed to have created in nature poetry an atmosphere in which one could distance oneself from the official literature of the Third Reich. The war broke in on them like a force of nature for many. It tore the illusions of an independent art to shreds. After the call-up, the arbour became desolate. All the writers were drafted, lost sight of each other, and Raschke was killed. But you remained in a state of aesthetic exaltation almost to the last. My father, Raschke and Lange went on writing (like most of the authors of their generation), without any difficulty in publishing their books. Martin Raschke offered the least resistance. As a war reporter, and before he died of a stomach wound, he wrote "TO A FRIEND" in the INNER REICH: 'A great fire is now ablaze. The furnace of fate, which seems to many people like a sacrificial altar to Moloch, is glowing like it hasn't for many a year. You entrust what you have shaped to the flames, all your beautiful vessels, what you think about death and about beauty, about regeneration and about the meaning of art, and you hope that the fire will temper it all and make it unbreakable. Weren't we all driving around with a cartload of unfired wares, not knowing properly what each particular vessel could do and what good they were? Now the fire has them. How many will crack in the heat! But what we get back, my friend, will be like a crystal formed in the fire and darkness of the earth, an inexhaustible wealth, a true cornucopia from fate. Such will be the true values. No, we are not luck's darlings, who toss any ballast aside carelessly and now must fear that the gathering storm will blast them off this fickle planet. We had the courage to commit ourselves to the fire, and by that I don't want you to understand just the thundering cannons, but each affirmation of the blessed hand of even the most terrible fate. Whatever in us has lasting worth, that will withstand the flames." (1943).

*

In the Thirties, Victor Otto Stomps's Raven Press was a literary centre in Berlin. The floor the publisher inhabited on the Landwehrkanal was famous for parties, drinking bouts and barrel organs; the atmosphere was brilliantly creative and, in contrast to the times, a clandestine anarchy, which slipped under the Third Reich's guard. The NSDAP[12] did not seem to notice. It was there that Oskar Loerke read his first poems (he was the last of the famous figures you still saw around); the poetry of Gertrud Kolmar[13] was printed there.

Stomps, the WHITE RAVEN, an unassailable personage, published young poets' first poems of (a pamphlet with my father's poetry appeared too), and then more and more others, which would not have been published otherwise. Munkepunke, Max Herrmann-Neisse, new Spanish poetry, poems by Mombert[14] and Jewish emigrés. In 1939, the Nazi press got wind of him and he was forced to sell his publishing house. He carried on his work with private printings; the few copies were given away to friends.

The end of the Raven Press came with the war. The White Raven was called up and made a career for himself. He disappeared as lieutenant-colonel amidst his Fatherland's war. Georg von der Vring[15] also became an officer. They were not ironclad patriots; their repugnance for the Third Reich was genuine. But they affirmed the military way; military virtues were beyond doubt; the honour of the German soldier was inviolable. A romanticising of Prussian tradition, patriotic youth-groups and second-hand ideals—they were uncritically at home in the German mentality. They did not feel at all bad in the barracks. I talked to both of them, Stomps and von der Vring, individualists, the proverbial DELECTABLE MOUNTAINS[16] and could only find out that that was how it was: a military career and the retreat into beautiful verses—the eerie ambivalence of a generation.

*

Extracts from my father's notes (I)

Speech by Hitler. Such a person stands at the head of Germany. (10.2.33)

Reichstag set on fire by Communists. Ominous revolutionary atmosphere and tension in the air. (28.2.33)

Eight o'clock. Police roadblock on the Laubenheimer Platz. Our house searched too. Arrest of Communists. Revolutionary atmosphere. (15.3.33)

In the evening a truly enchanting evening with Wilhelm Schäfer in the HJ[17] circle. Here you can sense something of the best spirit among young people. (23.1.38)

Wonderful evening with Carossa[18] in the Harnack House. (8.2.38)

Forebodings of dark things to come. (14.1.38)

Into town, books, radio, papers etc. Rain and dampness, unpleasant atmosphere, above all round the Alexanderplatz, mob against Jewish businesses. (24.6.38)

Finished reading Jünger's Wäldchen 125[19] gripped as never before by this elevated, spiritual depiction of war and by the disturbing descriptions. Jünger a wonderful mind. (28.6.38)

A man from the Party came wanting information about me and would like to get me into the Party. Refused. (9.9.38)

Phoned G. Serious discussion of our attitude to war. Who, if not we, can die decently? (14.9.38)

Heard speech by Hitler. Shaken by the undignified atmosphere, the sabre-rattling style of the message. (26.9.38)

Does Hitler want war? There is a repulsive, noisy rattling of sabres among us. Where dignity and the noble gesture? (12.10.38)

B. here in the evening, quite a few good discussions. We agreed that The People is basically something contemptible because it does remain spiritually no more than a mass. I am constantly aware how wonderful it is to go through life with Goethe, for instance. (2.1.39)

In the evening heard the Hitler speech on the radio, good, widely relevant and powerful. (30.1.39)

Otherwise, everybody is talking about war. I don't care, I have the present moment, no talk about politics.

6 a.m. woken by the warning siren, hear on the radio that it's war. I am collected and calm, think of my wife and children and gather around them all the good fortune and happiness in wishes that now seem redundant in my case. (1.9.39)

Depressed day. The decision to write nothing, not a word, not a line that could benefit from this war or further it. (26.10.39)

*

The future was already a few years old and seemed to be staying within acceptable bounds as far as he was concerned. He wrote poems, stories, anecdotes (the anecdote was considered a serious literary form in the Thirties) and published books with Cotta and the Inselverlag. At least once a week he went to the radio to get commissions. He wrote LITERARY PORTRAITS of the Nazi authors fêted by the State: Hans Grimm, Hans Johst, Guido Kolbenheyer[20] and Wilhelm Schäfer, took part in the annual writers' congress in Weimar and enjoyed (as he did later in the war) GOOD AND ABSORBING meetings there with Wilhelm von Scholz, Carossa,

Weinheber, Hans Grimm, Agnes Miegel and Ina Seidel, Waggerl, Wiechert and the Alemmanic BLOOD AND THUNDER BARD, Hermann Burte.[21] He published in anthologies of the day, together with writers who are now forgotten: Otto Brues, Fritz Diettrich and Adolf Georg Bartels.[22] He was a friend of Georg Britting, Albrecht Goes and W.E. Süskind,[23] respected Ernst Jünger and admired Josef Weinheber's lyric poetry. Weinheber's heroically resonant classicism confirmed his own intentions; its technical perfection was exemplary. The heady, nebulous thought of cultural circles in the Thirties, with concepts like HEREDITY, CLASSICISM, KINFOLK and LITERATURE AS THE NATION'S SPIRITUAL REALM, was filled up—by him too—with good faith once again. Nobility (in the human figure) was one of his tenets, and beauty (in language) was an inviolable value. He saw himself as the heir and DESCENDANT of the German Spirit and shared this conviction with Martin Raschke. "FOR US AS HEIRS", Raschke wrote, "and we don't wish to call ourselves anything else, there remains only the anxious preservation of the inheritance."

DON'T GAWP SO ROMANTICALLY! When a banner with this motto came down over a play by Bert Brecht, it was greeted as an aesthetic provocation, as a marvellously impertinent idea, but not understood as an exhortation to criticism. My father went on peering ahead through his romantic spectacles or looked unusually far into the past. He was, then, already living on the defensive, was programmed by authority (CANNON-FODDER) and did not suspect a thing. He read scarcely any political literature; the Communist Manifesto had no place in his library. He paid no attention to the recent world literature. He lived, thought, dreamed and wrote as if there had only ever been Goethe and Germany. Socialism and the Russian Revolution, the Spartacus uprising and the Spanish Civil War, the murder of Rathenau and the case of Ossietzky, the Moscow Trials[24] and Italian Fascism, unemployment and anti-Semitism—for him, all that never seemed to become quite real. Communism never seemed to enter his field of vision, to be discussed either positively or negatively. It was, quite simply, not part of his ménage. If he did notice anything like that, he saw it through the bourgeois liberal aesthete's lens (or smokescreen), that of someone whom history and world affairs scarcely touched. But also things much closer to home, literature—the Expressionist and Dadaist explosion, Majakowski[25] and socialist poetry, the literary-ideological discussions of the time (Marinetti, Tretjakow,[26] Benn etc.), the congresses for the defence of culture, French Surrealism, the new poetry from Spain and literature from America (much was translated and hence available)—he did not seem able to make anything of all that. There was scarcely any talk of politics—that was nothing rare for the Thirties. Such discussions were not opportune. Politics was the business of other people, all in all grubby artifice; you kept the realms of the spirit free from it. Hitler was a scandal for the homeland, a bogeyman, a noisy charlatan, not worthy of the Germans (they deserved better deliverers). The whole brownshirt movement was far too lacking in spirituality for him to have taken serious notice of it. The party was atrocious, vulgar and below consideration—yet not because of his political and critical insight but because of its political style. He did not like the style of the new authorities. Their approach was raucous, clattering and without dignity, and destroyed the most noble values of German culture. That could not be equated with Goethe and the Homeland. Anyone from among his friends who joined the party was laughed at until they resigned. Anyone who nevertheless remained a party-member could still sit round the table. My father was surrounded by Nazi literati and did not seem to think it important to keep a definite distance from them. The POWER OF THE SPIRIT still held good, and art was the main concern of a worthy existence. He had no contact with ideology, was not himself touched by it or called into question. He was determined to do nothing for the state. The criticism that he did utter seemed to stay within bounds. The appearances of the SA were infuriating, its uniform tasteless and comic, the stars of David an imposition and what happened to the Jews ("one heard nothing about it") awkward and embarrassing. Stupefied by the vapours from nationalistic clichés, ideologically unaware and uninterested in the economic foundations of the epoch, he lost himself ever more in the idea of the dignity of the spirit amid times without dignity.

He belonged to an unpolitical generation, counted himself among the spiritual elite and yet was only a typical epigone, one transported beyond prevailing circumstances by exhausted ideas: weak-winged high-flying, which only served to narrow his horizons still further. He did not seem to have any sense of his own narrowness. He was not the only blind man among his friends and he was not the only one to be carried along. He was surrounded by willing bearers and still more by those they were carrying; they surrounded him in their thousands. As a MAN OF THE SPIRIT he sat upright in the sedan chair of the master race and let himself be carried into the barracks. On the barrack square, he was hurled out of the sedan-chair; dignified and upright, he continued on foot, fled into an attitude of dutifulness and suffering and elevated it and himself into the notion of the Great Sacrifice. Weinheber's formula: "Nobility and Demise" defined what he seemed to expect: the destruction of those Germans with dignity by those without it.

In the period before the war it was impossible to ignore the fact that he was living in a dictatorship. He furnished his proof of Aryan descent and seemed to consider the business a farce. The ATMOSPHERE became dangerous. He received repeated visits from persons in civilian dress who wanted him to commit to the party—he refused. He rejected the request to cooperate in the CULTURAL PROPAGANDA of the NSDAP. The REICH CHAMBER OF LITERATURE was could not tempt him. There was a overseer for Schöneiche, one of the SS, who kept watch on him., Behind closed shutters and at night, he listened to the news on foreign stations with his friends. All that did nothing to alter his attitude.

Elitist inflexibility shielded his conscience.

*

Der Schnee fällt auf die Erde, um zu schlafen.
Er fällt, um auf der Erde zu schlafen.
Er fällt, um zu schlafen.

(The snow falls to earth to sleep.
It falls to sleep on the earth.
It falls, to sleep.)
(C. Meckel)

He believed in his talent and was still right to do so: it was productive. He worked reliably, gained acknowledgement from the critics and earned enough. He did not seem to lack anything. Private life held what he increasingly needed: bourgeois orderliness, dependable friends. You travelled to South Germany, to Thuringia or to the sea, played tennis with friends and went on skiing trips in the Müggelgebirge. He worked in the garden, read Goethe and Stifter and observed –imagining the Black Forest landscape—the night sky at all seasons through his telescope. His beautiful and clever wife was his total happiness. That she thought more precisely and saw more clearly, more critically, lived more painfully in the times, never quite seemed to dawn on him. The daily and nightly life of his house was more important than current events; the family and the support it brought him, his involvement with his child and with literature. His wish to go on unimpeded with what he had achieved. His patriarchal intent defeated any doubts. The first child was, as he had wished, a son; the firstborn had no right to be anything else but a son. In my father's rigid concept of family, only a son meant fulfilment, vindication, pride. He loved children and worshipped his own. As long as the child was innocent, before the onset of formal education (rules, instruction and what he called CORRECTION), he was an incomparable father, master of the revels, big brother, confidant and friend. He was the security, the rock and the fixed star; he was the unshakeable centre of childhood existence. His way of showing the world's phenomena entranced the child and enriched it. The path through the pines and the path to the fields, singing and whistling in the rain, all brought happiness. The friendliness of the sun, the sadness of the moon, the curiosity of the wind, the torpid snow. This father wanted to POSSESS THE HEART OF HIS CHILD, and he did possess it. The child was attached to the father and believed in him for a long time. He sat next to his father on a bench under the trees in the garden and listened to poems he read to him, Goethe's ballads and Eichendorff's verses. "Es scheinen so golden die Sterne,/ am Fenster ich einsam stand/ und hörte aus weiter Ferne/ ein Posthorn im stillen Land./ Das Herz mir im Leibe entbrennte,/ da hab ich mir heimlich gedacht:/ Ach, wer da mitreisen könnte/ in der prächtigen Sommernacht!" (The stars shone so golden, I stood alone at the window and heard from the distance a post-horn in the quiet countryside. My heart burned in my body and I thought to myself: Oh to be able to go with them in the superb summer night.)[27]

His voice floated away in a halftone somewhere between enthusiasm and melancholia. The child was captivated by the singsong of spoken verses. Disconcerting education via language. The hypnosis and the impact were so powerful that the child broke down in tears. Unrestrained weeping in an attempt to make the mysterious process bearable. The child wanted to save itself through its tears—and clung all the more tightly to the instigator of the poisoning.

That stable way of life lasted only a few years and was my father's best time. It was the best time for the child and it was the child's best time for him. Four years of almost boundless fulfilment. Then came (he had repressed the fear) the war. One morning it invaded the house, was an incomprehensible catastrophe and destroyed the personal—and also for a time the national—illusions of the bourgeois man of letters. His second child, a son, had been born, the fourth book, a volume of poetry, had been published. He was thirty-two years old. The call-up came, but the Inselverlag secured a stay of execution for its author. He was freed from the soldier's life for another year; the remittance of sentence was precious and unbearable, for whatever did not happen now, would not happen any more. He wrote a monograph on Conrad Ferdinand Meyer.[28] Once again he determined, amid his depressions, not to take any initiative that might support the Nazi State and this war. He still talked about decency in a degenerate age. In 1940 he was drafted, landed in the barracks in Strausburg as an infantryman, saw his home again on leave, less frequently during active service, and after the war never again. It was rented out, finally occupied by the Russians and badly damaged. The library was torn apart (the major part of it salvaged by removal to the west after the war). The family moved to a village near Freiburg. Your own home as a foundation stone for a lifetime, as a guarantee of the family's future, as a legacy to his children and a refuge in limbo—the dream remained an episode and perished with the end of the war.

*

Something had happened but what?

Presumably something terrible. A doctor came to the house, remained behind locked doors with my parents, went away without any explanation and nothing was like before. My parents spoke in a strange language (later I learned it was French).

What had the doctor and my parents been up to? What had become of the usual language we three shared? Even if it had been incomprehensible before, there were always some words I could understand. But the parents' language shut me out. Suddenly something was there that did not include me. Could there be anything that did not include me? Neither mother nor father wanted to explain anything. For the time being I was. in my anxiety, alone.

The doctor, my father's worries and this language—something did not add up any more.

After a few weeks a brother was born. Where did he come from? Inexplicable change.

*

Grown-ups would go to work on the children. Jackets were brushed and hair parted. Noses wiped and collars straightened. Children were created to be their parents' visiting card and had to make a faultless entrance. If visitors were in the house, late in the evening, the children used to be presented in the living-room, having been submitted to an examination in the hall, rapidly and soundlessly decked out in clean shirts, given a reminder, combed, and cleaned up around the corners of their mouth with their parents' saliva. Then they stood around for a while in the smoke and perfume, before the strangely delighted faces of the parents and their guests—actors, editors, and their wives—were observed, found to be excellent and were allowed to go.

If you wash it, a tomcat will shake himself. He rolls in the grass and goes on his way.

The childhood of the children belonged to the parents. Adults' hands pressed the children into shape; inescapable hands, the touching and tickling paws of strangers, hands for dressing and undressing, hands for slapping and fingertips that stroked. The arthritic, crippled hands of grandmothers and faded, soft, white, aunts' hands. Hands with rings and silver thimbles, scented ladies' gloves, the fists of the teachers. There were the damp and hard, laboriously tended hands of the maid and the plenipotent hands of the parents. There was the humourless index finger of the grandfather and the bridge-playing, knotted hands of strange men. The skin-and-bone hands of emotional greybeards and the innocuous, slapping hands of old spinsters. From the hands of adults came the sweets, the pocket money and unkind correction. Childhood—shrinking from adult hands, protest against all hands that did not lie gently on a child, against everything that was a hand and could not be shaken off.

*

Auf seinem Thron schlief der Despot,
Der jede Regung Geist verbot,
Wo's nur auf seinen Wink geschah,
Daß ihm der Mond durchs Fenster sah,
Wo sich kein Kater unterfing,
Daß er aus dem eignem Mausen ging.

(On his throne slept the despot who forbade
every new thought; only at his behest did the
moon look in at the window, and no tomcat took
the liberty of hunting mice on his own account).
(Oskar Loerke)

In grown-ups there lie hidden children: they want to play.

In grown ups there lie hidden officers: they want to punish.

In my grown-up father lay hidden a child whose play with his children was like heaven-on-earth.

There was lodged within him that sort of officer who wanted to punish in the name of discipline.

Pointless doting from the happy father. From behind the strewer of treats appeared an officer with a whip. He had punishments in store for his children. He directed a sort of punishment system, a whole programme. Initially there were scoldings and angry outbursts—that was bearable and passed over like a thunderstorm. Then came the pulling, twisting and pinching of ears, then the clip round the ear and the celebrated "Katzenkopf" slap on the back of your head. Banning from the room followed, and after that, incarceration in the cellar. And: the child-subject was ignored, humbled and shamed by a punitive silence. It was misused by being sent on errands, sentenced to bed or detailed to lug coal. Finally, as reminder and climax, there followed the punishment, the punishment proper, the exemplary punishment., That was the father's own measure, exclusive to him and applied by him implacably. In the name of Order, Obedience and Humanity, that justice might be done and that justice might impress itself on the child, a beating was administered. This species of officer seized the cane and went ahead into the cellar. Scarcely aware of his guilt, the child followed. He had to hold out his hands (palms upward) or to bend over his father's knee. The beating proceeded mercilessly and precisely, counted out loudly or softly and without remittance. This species of officer declared his regret at being forced to this measure, maintained that it pained him, as indeed it did.

The shock of the measure was followed by prolonged resentment: the officer prescribed cheerfulness. Pointedly cheerful, he led the way, set a good example in an oppressive atmosphere and was irritated when the child wanted no part of the cheerfulness. On several days, each time before breakfast, the punishment was repeated in the cellar. It became a ritual and the cheerfulness mere chicanery.

For the rest of the day the punishment was to be forgotten. There was no mention of guilt or penance, and right and wrong were blocked accounts. There was no cheerfulness from the children. Chalk-white, speechless or weeping secretly, brave, gloomy, sullen and bitterly perplexed they remained—even at night—prisoners of this righteousness. It pelted down on them, it got in the last blow, it had the last word from the father's mouth. This species of officer still punished whilst on leave and was depressed when his child asked him if he did not want to go back to the war now.

Children are swine, dirty little pigs and miniature criminals. They are mule-headed, deceitful, malicious and cunning and weigh sorely on their parents' hearts. They deliberately sit in the dirt, break pots, fiddle with the knobs on the radio without permission and ruin a car-heater. At times they are a veritable rabble; in the world of adults, they do their playing at their own risk. They were such disobedient little tomcats that they went mouse hunting off their own bat—in broad daylight. They could still learn from their mistakes, and they had to do too. Punishment helped to show the right way.

My faith in my father was breached for the first time when I was four.

I was taken along to the dressmaker. Whilst they draped my mother with materials on a little podium, turned her round, measured and advised her, endlessly offered advice, I was left to myself and my own games. The dressmaker's workshop had dark corners; there were tables with open drawers, material, chalk, all sorts of buttons and fat hedgehogs of pincushions. I found a ring in a bowl; it was a ring, nothing more, a round thing. This object pleased me and turned me into a criminal. With never a thought, I pocketed it. On the way home, my curiosity evaporated and I threw the ring down a grating in the street. On the same day there came a phone call: a valuable ring had disappeared and the child was suspected. I was summoned to my father and thoroughly interrogated. I had stolen an object of value and, above all, had put my parents into an embarrassing situation. I cast my mind back, came out with the information, and everything seemed all right: the ring was found under the grating and taken back by my parents.

The punishment followed in its heavy boots. For ten days, too long for any conscience, my father blessed the outstretched four-year-old palms of his child with a stinging cane. Seven raps daily on each hand: that makes one hundred and forty raps and a few more besides; it put an end to the child's innocence. Whatever happened in Paradise, with Adam, Eve, Lilith, the snake and the apple, the righteous Biblical thunderbolt from pre-history, the bellow of the Almighty and his finger of dismissal—I do not know anything about that. It was my father who drove me out of there.

III

Extracts from my father's notes (II)

I shall never become a soldier. (27.1.41)

Bad news from the East. Tripoli fallen too. Attacks on us from all sides. There's nothing else for it, we'll have to see it through. (23.1.43)

The tragedy of Stalingrad is over. The greatest defeat for the Fatherland in many years. Very grave and utterly painful. (3.2.43)

Trains full of Russians in indescribable state. Bloodless taking-over-and-apart of Europe by these hordes from the Steppes, apparently fleeing before the Bolsheviks. (17.1.43)

. . . worked on a talk, HISTORY AND NATURE OF BOLSCHEVISM. Very happy hours of activity trying to find the proper words . . . (15.4.43)

In the morning, officer-instruction, with my talk too. Special commendation from the Commander! (19.4.43)

To trial, long, wait. Case against a naturalised German, previously a Polish officer, who was a German lieutenant in Kavel, drank himself senseless and, made all sorts of mischief. Six months prison requested by me over and above the mandatory sentence. (22.6.43)

At 9 o'clock to Posen, very pleasant trip . . . In the Schloßcafé. Supper in the pleasant atmosphere of the Ostland Hotel. A young soldier decorated with the oak leaves,[1] infantryman; General Kluge. First-class, refreshingly urbane company. But as always, although I very much enjoy all that, my soldier's heart secretly despises it and wants to be away to the Front, to action and manly adventures. (30.6.43)

In the army bulletin, the evacuation of Palermo—and right there are Hohenstaufen graves,[2] with the English and the Americans standing over them now. Not easy to bear the thought. (24.7.43)

A column of 500 captive Italian officers, grotesque both to look at and to think about. Mostly severely ill with typhus. Begging cigarettes from the Poles, undignified. (3.10.43)

In the afternoon encounters with captured Italian officers; a colonel wants something from me and I allow him to come forward, so he climbs out of the carriage and approaches me. He complains, with the help of mangled German from a First Lieutenant, that it is not good to leave them almost without bread for five days. I counter that it is not good to be a Badoglio officer and am very short with him. I am more polite to another group of ostensibly fascist officers, who hold out all manner of papers to me, and have their carriage heated. (27.10.43)

Trouble with the cleaning women, who come and go just as they please. If you say anything to them, they reply: NO UNDERSTAN, thumb their noses and disappear. A wretched people. (21.1.44)

In the compartment, a woman, a civilian employee in Lemberg; she tells about a breakfast in a Warsaw pub that cost 4000 zloty, about the frauds and business methods of the Germans all through the administration. Bribes, overpricing and more of the same, about the camp in Auschwitz etc.—But as a soldier you really are distanced from all these things, which basically don't interest you anyway; you stand for another sort of Germany out there and don't want later to have grown rich from the war, but to have a sense of remaining unsullied. I have nothing but contempt for this civilian rubbish. You are perhaps stupid, but soldiers are always the stupid ones who have to pay. Nevertheless, we have a code of honour that no one can steal. (24.1.44)

Taking a long way round to lunch, witness the shooting of 28 Poles, which takes place publically on the terraces of a sports field. Thousands line the streets and the banks of the river. A jumbled pile of corpses, yet a sight that leaves me absolutely cold despite its horror and squalor. Those shot had ambushed and killed two soldiers and a naturalised German. Shape of popular theatre in the new age. (27.1.44)

*

I had not intended to spend time on my father. It did not seem necessary to write about him. His case, a private case, was closed. I might have noted down memories of him without any intention of making anything out of them. I would probably not have thought about him much longer. Nine years after his death, he comes back again and reveals his profile. Since I read his war diaries, I cannot let his case rest any longer; it is no longer private. I found the notes of a person I did not know. It was not possible to know this person, to deem him possible—inconceivable. What I did know about his Nazi phase, I only knew from his own accounts. That was the laundered version of his role, all in all an uncontroversial choice of words. It went without saying that nothing had actually been as harmless as he claimed; doubt still remained. There was his lyric poetry and prose from over 20 years; the nationalistic tendency was undeniable. But in spite of it all, there was no reason to deem any other person possible apart from the existing, well-known one. The person I knew, or thought I knew, was only a part of that other one, whom no one knew. Now that I have got to know the one and the other, there simply is not any daily routine to which I can move on.

He was stationed as a corporal in Lodz. Apart from all sorts of periods of leave, into which his hopes for a future life compressed itself (he even went to the Black Forest for a few days), he was a soldier and became one more and more. He went up the ranks as far as lieutenant over his three years of service . . . The stations of his military career (with special postings and training) were Warsaw, Wilna, Witebsk, Brest-Litowsk, Minsk, Kutno and Orel. On weekends, he took trips into the accessible countryside of Poland. Although he dreamed repeatedly of a posting to the front, he remained a staff officer almost to the end.

The beginning was terrible. He did not succeed in adapting. The break with civilian life, and more so with his family, seemed insurmountable (the pressure to enter the Party abated—that was the only advantage in his situation). The masculine world of the barracks was scarcely bearable. Daily drill reduced the spiritual and elitist individual to a common recipient of orders. The monotonous grinding into shape eroded his will and depressed him. The sterility of years of guard duty: guard at the Division and the barracks, guard on the depot, guard on the army stadium and on the railway yards. He memorised constellations and poems and dreamed himself back into his home countryside. Being a soldier meant functioning, he functioned. Functioning meant mounting guard; you remained standing where you stood. Inner discipline was a matter of honour. Of himself, he demanded self-control and kept his outbreaks of despair for the nights. At least he could be alone on guard duty.

He was a dependable comrade. Comradeship became for him, as for all of them, the watchword that kept the misery in check. It became an internal ideology. On the strict basis of EQUAL AMONG EQUALS, he got along with all his comrades; he respected many of them and was respected by many. He read out poems on mess-evenings. His pensive caste of mind, with its nationalistic undertones, was received sympathetically; it gave the dismal drill a tinge of meaning. It dispensed solace and soothed men's feelings. He reinforced the others in doing their duty.

He worked his way out of the grey beginnings. The eternal drill was difficult for him, but in weapons training he showed all sorts of skill. In classes on military theory he stood out thanks to what he already knew and to his commitment. The ideological schooling suited him. He was, as a spiritually inclined German, predestined for the progress towards a Greater Germany. On the shooting range he proved himself a brilliant marksman. SCHOOLBOY PLEASURE in shooting, in the chance of a record and a sporting contest. The meaning of the training (killing, destruction of the enemy) did not seem to occur to this romanticist. He was praised by the Captain and liked it. He did the daily duty and was good at it, then better than good, and then, after a year and a half, took pride in it.

Years of soldier's life on the general staff. The German army was fighting across half of Europe—and so he would rather have been at the Front. The time passed amid military routine, Poland meant boredom and stagnation. However, he also saw the opportunities and took them. Any risk to his own life remained limited. You lived in a ambience that was halfway German, had private access to German families, to all kinds of CULTIVATED SOCIETY—birthdays, feast days and musical evenings. You frequented the theatre and restaurants, officers' messes, football fields, stage reviews and films. You celebrated, got drunk to the degree proper for the German occupier. The German soldier represented a Master Race. He set an example on enemy soil.

He rarely had to do with Poles. The contact limited itself to conflicts with cleaning women and partisans. Everything else was experienced by looking on. He saw the poverty and vastness of Poland with a mixture of hubris and fascination. Eastern Europe seemed strange to him; he sought everywhere for reminders of home: the old churches, the villages and inn-gardens. That was where he liked to linger at the weekends. He viewed the poor districts and the ghettos from the prescribed military perspective; that was the degenerate state of a bygone age, the new age would clear away such relics. It would take a while until the Poles were worthy of the Germans; there was still a lot to do. Meanwhile, the eastern soul had to suffer (one was NOT INHUMANE and tried to understand); the severe German occupation was difficult to bear, but the situation was unavoidable and whoever surrendered his dignity was lost. The children formed the exception to all that. He loved children, even if they were Polish.

He withdrew as often as possible from his surroundings and wrote poetry. Wherever he wound up, he erected his idyll, wrapped in a cocoon of contemplation. He read the classics and Moltke's[3] writings and noted every MOOD OF THE SEASON—the sound of the rain on the barracks roof, the colours of the summer sky over the ghetto. In such withdrawal, he preserved a minimum of private continuity. There, writing his letters, he surrendered to homesickness. The war was bad enough (it had to be, of course), but worse was the separation from his wife. Greatness and Decline of the Fatherland (the political illiterate did not see the reasons) meant little compared with the fact that his children were growing up without him. In everything he thought and did, he kept rigidly to the responsibilities prescribed for a soldier. Here he was safe from possible misgivings (and any deeper doubts did not seem to assail him). It was his appointed station and his personal dignity. There was scarcely any talk of politics, seldom with comrades and officers, still less with his wife while on leave. Faith in the legitimacy of the war, unconditional trust in authority, a reduction of thinking to set principles, that all made any ambivalent feelings melt away. Amid it all, he lacked the elementary sense of horror because he lacked insight into the overall context.

He accommodated himself, and I wonder what that means. He adjusted to things, he co-operated.

The necessary precondition lay in his determination to succeed in a situation which did not seem to suit his nature. He adjusted (he secured his position), initially as a subject of authority. He was able to adjust because authority was a fixed point he never questioned. Authority was a phenomenon he affirmed through a very subtle, scarcely perceptible form of submission. He had already—through his behaviour and his nature— always affirmed all manner of things. He had affirmed his father, after that his Fatherland and various other things too. (He would have accommodated himself to everything, even to a bloody dictatorship; he would have submitted, albeit in bitterness, and would have criticised at most the way blood was spilled but not the bloodletting itself; where blood was spilled, that had meaning; the meaning of the bloodletting was something pre-established). He adjusted to it; he accommodated himself, that was the precondition for the next step. Now he was almost ready to make a career. A further step: having a voice in military matters. Exercising command, so he wrote, was enjoyable.

Accommodating oneself can be inevitable. Within limits, he could not avoid it. It was vital for everyone who was on the defensive, and how much more vital for the persecuted, those openly discriminated against, the prisoners in the camps. You accommodated yourself in order to survive and never forgot why you did it. Self-accommodation could mean camouflage; it was ruled by cunning and intelligence. Without techniques of pretence, without mimicry and deception, half of humanity would not have survived. Yet the art of self-camouflage with integrity, not determined by indolence but by intent, was not his way; he was no Schweyk.[4] He did, in actual fact, accommodate himself diligently, first of all as an infantryman and later on as an officer, and he did it with the utter conviction of being in the right and not with an eye to the end of the war. He sang and marched in unison with the German Reich (but not at all with Hitler, S.S. or Nazi Party); he affirmed expansionism by force of arms. He believed in the triumph of the German Idea and felt the retreat (the CRUMBLING as he called it) as a painful loss for himself and his homeland. He adjusted in anticipation of a future that would be just, German and everlasting. He accommodated himself within the embodiment an idea. His identification with it was meant to last a whole life.

He was no longer merely subject to authority: he was an officer. He had the others as subordinates: he was authority. The minute authority stood at his disposal, to use or abuse, the extraordinary change appeared. He progressed to the role of a superior and left the weaknesses and strengths of self-accommodation behind. His share of power was rather limited—it sufficed to eradicate his sensitivity. He was not a natural wielder of power, he became one by conviction. Soldierly title and rank were his watchwords. The comradeship and duty required of a soldier were monitored by him with utmost severity. In the past he had despised the man who kicked over the traces, became a drunk and a deviant and did not conform to the image of the German soldier. Now he was empowered to prosecute such cases. He prosecuted them with unalloyed justness. This sort of justness could work FOR THE MAN and it could work AGAINST THE MAN. It still wanted, in his case, to remain comradely. He could, either privately or officially, stand on his own fairness and rescind a punishment, with pronounced generosity (WE ARE COMRADES). He could make a visible point of turning a blind eye. He let a couple of Polish coal thieves go and saved a drunkard from close confinement. Such a deed was not pure humanitarianism. It was simply the pointedly humane exercise of his personal authority.

Authority changed his viewpoint. The aesthete concerned with refined language now descended increasingly to the toilet-wall slang of the Master Race. He was perhaps not a misanthropist, but now he saw pollacks, wretched sluts and surly rabble everywhere. He was very likely no anti semite, but he regarded the disposal of the Jews as fate, a terrible tragedy for the individual but on the whole ineluctable. He looked on the bullet-riddled enemy without interest. The slain partisan did not disturb his peaceful dreams.

The thin aesthetic shell began to crack. The brutalisation of the officer increased. The chauvinism of the underling-in-authority became apparent. He had forgotten what he had been at the beginning; he won a competition for soldiers' poetry. He held courses on ballistics and ideology, was ambitious in running them and earned praise. He functioned beyond what was required of him. The recurring melancholia made no difference.

*

He lived, in Lodz, in the house of deported Jews. That would have bothered him earlier (or so I hope: it would have bothered him, cost him his sleep, spoiled his appetite). The officer was immune to all that. The German officer lived there legitimately, no question about that. One friend spent his leave in the apartment and discovered utensils left behind by the Jews in the kitchen cupboard. This friend, seized by insight and despair, hurled crockery against the wall. My father was piqued and let it be known that he did not understand such fits; one had transcended such outbursts by now.

He had transcended them, for a few years.

*

In Spring 1944, he was promoted to First Lieutenant and posted to the island of Elba, an important German strongpoint in the Mediterranean with a garrison of three thousand men and heavy artillery. He took up a position near Marina die Campo on the west coast with forty Italian and German troops. What he wanted was there again: stationed in an idyll amid the war. Air raids and DARK FOREBODINGS disturbed the lethargic military routine, but the nights were warm and there was nothing to do. At most, patrols through the maccia,[5] searches of remote villages for weapons, partisans and deserters, obtaining supplies and attending briefings on the mainland. He seemed to have been considered a friendly "Tenente".[6] Farmers on the island turned to him and he forestalled the order to evacuate their houses. All the rest was the South and the summer, bucolic life, enjoying a breather and writing letters, rowing in cliff-edged bays and swimming in the sea; dreams under pines, siesta and wine.

Two months later, the phoney peace was over. At dawn on 17 June the allied invasion began. Supported by the Royal Navy and the U.S. Air Force, a BATTALION DE CHOC landed on the beach directly in front of his position—three thousand Senegalese in landing craft. With forty troops he defended his strongpoint against a few hundred blacks. Capitulation was not an option for him. His mentality committed him to hold out at any cost. IN THE BITTER FULFILMENT OF HONOUR AND DUTY FOR THE FATHERLAND. He scratched the sentence into the concrete wall of his bunker (years later he came back as a tourist, photographed the writing on the wall and memorised WITH EMOTION THE SITE OF THE DEFEAT). A proportion of the Germans and a larger proportion of the Italian troops died; he himself defended the strongpoint to the last. As the lone survivor, lying in a hole in the cliff, he fired on heads and uniforms. A Senegalese (he even saw the man) shot him in the head, just past the left temple. He was unconscious when the French captured him. The invasion was over after twenty hours. Gardens by the sea full of wrecked weapons and mutilated Negroes. He came round in a camp on the coast and wanted to kill himself—a leap through the broom bushes onto the rocks by the sea. The thought of his wife and children restrained him. Whilst a few hundred dead disappeared into mass graves, he lay on a stretcher and dozed.

He was transported to Corsica in a consignment of badly wounded German and French soldiers. On the subsequent journey by lorry through the mountains, he thought he was going to die. Agonising pain under the emergency dressing, loss of sight and frequent fainting. A French nurse held his hand. The warmth and stability of a living hand saved his life; he still talked about it years later.

There followed two months of hospital in the citadel of Corté. The operation on his head was a success, but splinters remained and the healing dragged on. It took him some time to come to himself again. He was isolated and had nothing to read. Conversations with Arabs, Corsicans and wounded Germans, wandering the rooms behind barred windows, the view of chestnut trees in the mountains, wind in the rooms of the fortress, in the leaves of the chestnuts—everything else was torpor, confusion and pain.

Two months later, distracted and sick, he was transferred to the central prison in Ajaccio. From there a general transport of captive officers went on to Algiers, on the deck of the City of Ajaccio (25000 tons) amid neglect, heat and apathy. The transportation became for him a sea voyage coloured with Homeric reminiscences, then came nonexistence in the desert. The prisoners were herded through Algiers to the railway station and then shipped off in hellishly hot wagons. A thousand kilometres on the rails, through the Sahara, southwards to Géryville, the biggest French camp for German prisoners. He arrived exhausted beyond measure. On entering his allotted barrack, he sensed, gratefully, something like HOME again.

AT LAST, A REAL REFUGE.

*

THE OPERATION ON HIS HEAD WAS SUCCESSFUL, BUT A FEW SPLINTERS OF BONE REMAINED BEHIND. That was the sort of formula I heard whenever his HEAD INJURY was mentioned.

The actual state of affairs looked different and you avoided talking about it. The injured man did not want to hear any talk about illness. BRAIN DAMAGE was a contemptible term. It was replaced by head or war injury.

The hospital in Corté was primitive. He lay on the operating table and looked up into a fly-spotted lamp. The bullet had ripped open 18 centimetres of his skull. The surgeon (known to hate Germans) did not seem to take any particular trouble: he removed the accessible bone splinters. In the course of healing, lesions formed. His brain attached itself to them and could no longer float freely; the results plagued him for the rest of his life: headaches, speech impediment, obtuseness and pressure inside the skull; a change in the weather and the Föhn brought severe afflictions. He came back from the war a changed man, and the question everyone concealed from him was: had the brain damage changed his nature or just brought out weaknesses which, although concealed, had always been there.

Presumably it was a case of both at once. He was irritable, restless and constantly tense. A shutter was left open by mistake, a shoe had disappeared, a book gone missing—that was a terrible thing. He lost control of himself in states of extreme agitation, which bore no relation to their cause. And what fears tormented this man who claimed to fear nothing! He had always been threatened by fears (fears determined his behaviour in the war), now they could no longer be hidden. At night he lay sleepless until everyone was back in the house, and being alone only seemed bearable for him if he knew when it would be over.

*

As I think about him, he becomes a theme. The sentences bear him way into formulations that simultaneously illuminate and obscure his outline.

To write about someone means: destroying the reality of their life in favour of the reality of words. The syntax demands that whoever is dead has to die all over again. Destroying them and creating them amounts to the same procedure. But I do not want to assert my rights over my theme.

What remains from a living person? What comes to light about them through the mechanism of the sentences? Perhaps a sense of his character, the fleeting or firm contours of a picture puzzle. It cannot be done without invention. I have not invented anything about his personality, but I have selected and compiled (depicting without judging is not possible). I have made sentences, that is to say: invented language.

The invention reveals and conceals the human being.

IV

Géryville lies 1300 metres above sea level in the Atlas mountains, on a plateau on the fringes of the rocky desert. The winter brings frost and snow; the storms are cold. The summer is hot with distinctly cool nights. The differences in temperature are dangerous. One adopted the Arabs' habits, wore a waistband, something to cover your head and warm socks and did not linger unnecessarily in the sun. Sandstorms would peck at the barracks for days and nights on end. Dust devils hissed through the sparse grass. The barbed wire sang.

On the edge of an oasis inhabited by the Arabs there rises up the fortress of EL BAJJATH, a former legionnaires' post dating from 1853, a bulwark of stone, impregnable, with barracks, officers' and administrative blocks, parade grounds and casemates. Next to it, the prisoners' barracks arranged in a square. From the top of the ramparts, the view out into the oasis, over waves of sand to mountain crags in the changing light. The monotonous panorama had an oppressive effect, above all on cloudless days. The empty blueness fostered depressions; the sirocco and the light reinforced latent psychoses. Screaming in the night, cabin fever, suicide. You did not become habituated to the sight of the sky and land; a pompous sunrise brought little pleasure. Winter in the barracks was cool and healthy. The hot season brought dropsy, jaundice, fever and diarrhoea.

The food, one of the main things in such an existence, tended towards the bad rather than the good and was cursed on principle. Prisoners received 300 grammes of bread, pumpkin soup or overcooked noodles, some tomatoes or beans in addition, only rarely meat. Occasionally dried fishes turned up; they were small and tasted of nothing but salt. The prisoners invented a SMOKEHOUSE made of old barrels and enhanced their fishes (five per head) into something like European-tasting sprats. It was possible to barter and trade in the camp; packages came—not often—from German relatives; there were donations of foodstuffs from the Red Cross and, varying according to season and chance, the wares of a French sutlery: sticks of cocoa, concentrated jam, dates, tobacco and wine.

Sometimes a couple of gulps of cognac from a Europe-package.

Every day children came from the oasis. They stood begging between the sentries at the fence, and the prisoners threw scraps of bread to them through the barbed wire.

Outside was the oasis and hence life, people and animals, the fires of Ramadan, singing at night and the clapping of Arab soldiers. Out there were the nomads (camels and tents), Berbers with their horses, and Bedouins, Turks, Kabylians, Spaniards and Tuaregs, Moroccans and Indians.

There were cedars, palms, olives, tamarisks. Acacias, mescal, coffee trees, oleander. There was cotton grass, camel thorn, thistles, cacti. Melons and mandarins, so the word went.

There were vultures, eagles, bee-eaters and flying foxes. Bullfrogs, cuckoos, storks and screech owls, larks, antelopes and swifts. Gerbils. Wildcats. Sparrow hawks. Jackals.

In the camp there were fleas, bedbugs, mosquitoes, snakes, ants and scarab beetles, at most a few lizards or crickets; several times huge swarms of locusts descended on them.

Sometimes, very high, a bird of prey over the camp.

On the wind, a scent of lamb and unknown seasonings.

At night, a barking and whimpering in the desert.

Now and then, the jingling of a lone tin bell.

For years on end, he did not see any women.

*

Extracts from my father's notes (III)

Miserable betrayal of the misled people by its leaders. No one ever listened to the intelligentsia. So we have to carry the can when it's the others who are to blame. (30.4.45)

Spent a long time watching the swallows that nest in our housing and play their games of loving and flying. Time does not bother them. (9.5.45)

Have read a lot, above all Hölderlin: Hyperion,[1] the language of which gripped me powerfully. Goethe, Hölderlin, Stifter, these really are the limits of my world. (9.6.45)

Love and reverence must be reinstated in order to preserve European values. (August 1945)

*

He lived in captivity for three years. He suffered circulatory disorders and heart trouble—all in all a lesser evil. Various after-effects from his head injury put him into hospital several times (there he took his first bath for one and a half years). He administered the camp library and occupied himself with the CULTURAL WELFARE of his fellow-prisoners. Alongside theatre, orchestra and university (prisoners' initiatives without any support from the French), the library was a centre for SPIRITUAL SUSTENANCE. He organised readings of classical literature from Hölty[2] to Weinheber on anniversaries and feast days, or of his own volition. The interest—among the French too—was so strong that the readings regularly had to be shifted into bigger rooms.

The issuing area, a room in the barracks, was open every day except Sundays. It was too much for a severely injured man, but it secured him one vital privilege: retreat from the miseries of the camp routine. He was alone there, surrounded by books and had time for private matters. He purged the library of Nazi literature, catalogued the newly arrived books donated by the Red Cross—three thousand in two and a half years –and drew up suggested reading for beginners and for advanced readers. He agonised over poems, worked on novellas, failed at a novel (THE LOST

DECADE) and wrote notes about his own self.

He had time now, as much as he wanted; he had time as never before. Time stood still, outweighing everything else; it was the only luxury amid chronic shortages. It came out of the desert, crept past the camp clock and scorned every roll call. You lived on a joyless MAGIC MOUNTAIN (Thomas Mann's novel was the most read book),[3] bottled up behind barbed wire, in a WAITING-ROOM MENTALITY, stalled in a grey monotony. There was no need to steal time; it came to every card game and played a hand. You took it outside and killed if off or, like a sullen phoenix, turned it into ashes. Time was there and offered its help.

He preferred to be alone as surviving was easier that way. He undertook a thorough therapy of self-education. Everything in print was welcome. He went through Schiller again, Gryphius[4] and Hölderlin, read literary or historical tomes and occupied himself with botany and zoology. He read scientific publications (the example of Ernst Jünger hovered in the background), taught himself about the fundamentals of chemistry and noted formulae. He looked into Kretzschmar's typology,[5] found it credible and applied it to himself. Art-history, foreign languages, philosophy, Leibnitz, Schopenhauer and Hegel's works,[6] Bismarck's letters and Rosegger's novels.[7] Sociology and French essays. Atomic physics and the theory of Bolshevism—he lifted the weight of time from his soul by reading and went to sleep over his books.

In writing, and still more so in reading, he held onto his sense of self. He never again came so close to knowing himself. He had lived his whole life as a cultivated bourgeois, one exalted and fulfilled by Great Literature. He remained a cultivated reader and an idealist, who noted aphorisms, drew sustenance from proverbs, found solace in maxims and appreciated profundity. But out there that was not enough. For once in the four stages of his life, he found a critical perspective on himself. That meant exposing himself to dangerous insights. He noted the lack of real kindliness, recognised what was PROBLEMATICAL in a lifetime's self-isolation—now further intensified by confinement in the camp. He sensed CERTAIN CONSTRICTIONS in his being, restrictions of his character and the tendency to repress things. Later the awareness dimmed; the—relatively sharp—illumination of his own self got lost amid everyday concerns. But for a few moments the insight was there. He learned it by heart, inwardly digested it, systematically, like a conscientious student in a seminary. For weeks, he managed to, as it were, pass through the mirror. There he confronted—INWARDLY MOVED—the insight that there was such a thing as German collective guilt. He accepted his share and did not try to minimise much. Collective guilt did not crush him; he almost found a home in it. But personal guilt—NO. He had wanted what was worthy and had done his best. Personal guilt was not open to debate. That was pre-empted by his civil courage, by the HONOUR OF A SOLDIER, the betrayal of western culture, and the greatness of art. Now he could not repeat the leap to the other side. The admirer of Moltke did not want to remember how he had adopted a Prussian mentality. Albert Schweitzer's idea of the FELLOWSHIP OF THOSE MARKED BY SUFFERING[8] made an opportune appearance and embraced him.

He had not been a National Socialist, that much he could now claim, and it made enemies for him. That was something he could also embellish for his own use. It gained him friends among the French administration of the camp and trusty fellow-conspirators among the other prisoners. At the weekends, you went to his office; there were conversations, wine and a gramophone. His first sense of release dawned there, and it was there, and only there, among the kindred souls, that laughter reappeared. It was still a tentative laughter, but it worked. It was—and thanks for asking—working again after all. By then, you could read the first accounts of the slaughter, Auschwitz and Oradour—the horror came rather late. The righteous indignation brought no pleasure, did not pacify your conscience, did not get you any further. The great release did not happen according to plan, and there was no happy ending to the pent up desire for guiltlessness. He now knew and was, for a moment, sobered. His personal honour and the dignity of the spirit became his lifelong guidelines.

*

Contradictory reports of the situation in Germany, rumours of release with denials of them, and rumours about transfers to other camps turned the years into a permanent war of nerves. The oscillation between exaltation and apathy. The lack of sympathy from the French was proverbial. Seven hundred Arab soldiers, French officers and specialists (doctors, priests, cooks, administrators) confronted the prisoners with more or less indifference.

His susceptibility to depression paralleled a strong need for INNER RESTORATION. He grasped after every straw. The sight of the night sky in the Sahara, a maxim from Schopenhauer or the MANLY ATTITUDE to his situation, which he felt to be one of GREATNESS IN ADVERSITY. He eschewed, as far as that was possible, masculine jokes and intrigues and restricted himself to his few fellow-spirits. Among themselves they spoke of PRIDE UNDER TRAGIC CIRCUMSTANCES, stressed their sense of responsibility for Germany's future and maintained HUMAN RIGHTS in opposition to battledress mentality. The pact helped them through their existence as castaways en masse. Profession and background played no role. Even more than during the war, class differences lost any meaning. Lawyers, doctors, aristocrats and artists, masons, tailors and career-officers, family men and homosexuals came together in the common striving to SURVIVE DECENTLY. Whilst the camp roads dissolved into mud under the desert storms, next door they swayed to songs from home. You listened to classical music, sought intoxication in Chopin and took NOBLE GERMAN ART as a reason for a sentimentalised heroising of your situation. For many, much became unbearable. The bedbugs, the time-wasting and the boredom were unbearable. The unchanging exhalations of the masculine existence were unbearable. Yet more unbearable was the lack of privacy in the barracks. Packages, news, and each one's business were commandeered by the rest. Love letters lost their appeal under remorseless questioning. Nothing and no one escaped comment. To preserve some dregs of private life, you fled into mystification. You took on the guise of a misanthropic oddity, feigned illness or stayed silent. Years later, you happened to find out how, in those days, one friendly fellow-prisoner, Otto Franzen, had had a child killed in the bombing and had no wife any more.

*

He had salvaged a few family photos, postcards and German newspaper clippings. He still possessed three old letters from his wife and a few scribblings from his children. For years he carried a photograph of a Black Forest pine around with him. The remains of a hiker's map did duty for the rest of the world.

*

For months he had no news of his family. Thoughts of misfortune were repressed. French press reports and rumours in the camp only recounted the destruction of Germany. Freiburg was, like most German cities, destroyed. Uncertainties, those already existing and new ones daily, made any hopeful anticipation a farce. Solace and hope were on the rack. Months of heart trouble led to relapses into his childhood complaint: lack of breath and speech impediment. He missed the solace of being loved more than the others did. His homesickness was painful.

For two years, his name stood on the list for repatriation. For two years he was put back without any explanation. He watched others go and remained behind. The lost time could not be made up any more. Innate melancholia turned into depression, which had him again in its close and dismal grip. The self-imposed inner and outer tenacity became a despairing tour-de-force; at best he stared STEADFASTLY INTO THE DARKNESS. The dream of his family kept him alive (he wrote a novella to stave off suicide). Later on, it was scarcely possible to imagine how he had survived the limbo.

*

Through indirect channels, by way of Switzerland, he received the news that his family was alive. The miracle of this certainty brought new doubt: there was nothing in the news to tell him in what circumstances they were living. Whilst he kept himself going on the fact that they were alive, they had gone in their homelessness from Freiburg to Erfurt, had learned a short while before that he was alive (he had been declared missing for a few months) and hoped for news through the Red Cross. The mother was living with the three children in her parents' house on the edge of town, in a quarter favoured by civil servants. Hunger, anxiety and cramped living space made the post-war years into a sinister adventure. The writing on the wall read: go on living and forage. The mother foraged (the children foraged along with her) for potatoes, turnips, nettles and elderberries, the remains of vegetables from fields already plundered ten times over, hot brew (a cloudy liquid), molasses and fat. Whenever she went on her foraging, she had a child by her for protection. I evolved into a good and quick thief; I stole chocolate from American jeeps and ripped the last of the wood from the changing-cubicles of a nearby stadium. One summer evening, the gun club building, which was full of military equipment, was opened up for plundering. I ran there with my grandfather; thousands of others were there before us. The public rooms rang with the din; we carried off boots and uniforms, rolls of cellulose (a material without any possible use), whole boxes of iron crosses, which we swapped for lard or corned beef (the German decoration had a high value as a souvenir among the U.S. soldiers, above all with the blacks). The forests were full of wrecked tanks and empty of wood. Whoever transgressed by sawing at a tree had to reckon with an exemplary sentence. Saws and axes were clandestine possessions. Dusk every day swarmed with human silhouettes engaged in lifesaving felony. You fled to bed from hunger and cold. You survived your exhaustion by lying there. Children roasted mice on secret fires, but the slippery corpses were inedible. I threw them into the rubble and dragged myself off home.

As a result of the allied agreements at Yalta (February 1945), some American-occupied parts of Germany were surrendered to the Soviet Union. For days, we sat in the neighbours' kitchen, pondering, hoping, shooing doubt away. Would the border run to the east of Erfurt? Calculations according to the map brought no certainty. Erfurt lay at the centre of the shift from west to east. The American occupiers, chewing their gum and lying on their vehicles, withdrew westwards in convoys of jeeps and trucks that lasted days at a time. I stood by the long highroad, amid the rumble of tanks, and was told by gloomy voices that the end of the safe times was at hand. One day remained free for hoping and fearing, the stillness of that one day was worse than the war. Whoever ran to the neighbours through the hole in the fence thought they had terrible things to fear. Nothing happened. Fear stood behind closed windows and waited without a sound. The whole world seemed like something left behind and was waiting without a sound, like the soundless cherry tree belonging to the milkman next door. I sat on the veranda and, with baited breath, for twelve hours looked at nothing: an empty street. Next morning THE RUSSIANS were there. They came in their thousands from the Thuringian forest, with their panje carts,[9] their greasy uniforms, their bald skulls that bespoke the steppes: Asiatic bogeymen. The shaven heads gleamed dully, a flecked, leaden blue. I stood by the same long highroad, now ringing with the clatter of hooves, watched the advance of a ramshackle army and was told by gloomy voices that the dangerous times had come. They came with their thefts, attacks, arrests, curfews, rapes and shooting in the nights. Trampling Russians brought RAIDS on the house and caused what was still left to disappear: bicycles, clocks, lamps, porcelain. At night roving bands of Polish and Czech marauders took revenge on exhausted households by plundering them. Our maid Lucie, in the family for years, went past the gates of the barracks and disappeared without trace. Orgies of dangerously drunk officers; naked women ran into the street. I saw: there were women who got big bellies. My grandmother did the washing for Russian families and was paid with army bread. The bread was dirty and had to be cleaned. It was scrubbed in hot water, dried by the stove and eaten APPRECIATIVELY. The fear left over from the war disappeared under the greater fear of the uncertainty brought by THE RUSSIANS. They confirmed, right down to the hairs on their heads, the spectre that fear and prejudice had transmitted. They washed in the toilet bowl, wrecked the doors and windows, and snored head downwards on the stairs. Germans were dragged from their beds, driven off in jeeps and did not return. Dead Russians lay by the fence in the mornings, were shoved into sacks and hauled away. The Russian night was terrifying; it seemed to me a sham copy of the natural night. There were noises in it that I did not know yet. It was as if the animals in the gardens, the cats and the birds, had gone across to the Russians. The world outside, the stillness and the darkness were not in tune. That could be unmasked by a noise at any moment. Running feet on the footpath, casual steps in boots, marching boots, the curses of men, above all, the scream of a woman. Whimpering in an apartment not far from me. Nothing was more terrifying than the scream of a woman. It meant something was being done to a lone person, and that was more terrible than an air-raid warning. The chance of a miracle was gone forever. Childhood ended in grey chaos.

In exchange for the clothes of an uncle killed in action, we at one point acquired—through a discreet channel of negotiation—a whole hundredweight of coal. The stoker in a Russian barracks shovelled it aside little by little. Grandfather, his partner in the deal, and the eldest child heaved it over the barracks wall one night (outside stood the handcart, worth its weight in gold). It was pulled unnoticed through empty streets, was already in the garden, and we were heaving a sigh of relief, when a cobbler, who was billeted in the house, blackmailed us through a crack in the door by threatening denunciation. Grandfather's dumb rage did not help us. For weeks two-thirds of our good fortune warmed the cobbler's lair.

A few months after the Americans had first arrived, there ensued the first mass release of German prisoners from American camps. On the same highroad, not far from our house, the figures of those released passed by for weeks on end: limping, weeping, starving, helped along by comrades, the dour remnants of human beings, alone and in groups. Thousands in shuffling misery, the wounded on crutches, surviving on fresh air and their own momentum, picking berries at a garden fence, barefoot, in cut-off trousers and bloody rags. I stood at the roadside every day with the job of asking after my father. No one knew anything about releases by the French. Individual soldiers claimed to know something. I dragged them into the house and they sat there, plagued with questions from grandmother, mother and child—without result. They had not come to give information but to be fed potatoes.

Washed and sated, they disappeared down the highroad. We found out nothing about my father.

*

He withdrew into his barrack and made notes.

He had nothing, he wanted to have something. His memory bored into his past and drew the life he lacked into the present. His memory of himself ran though all its phases and discovered an eerie scheme for his notes: he created the list. What had been hope, homeland and love, disappointment, breath, openness, maelstrom and dream, it all disappeared, noted as names, into his list. He had time and occasionally paper too. Paper, time and here and now for his list.

An extraordinary general meeting of his people. All the dead and living on the list. What a system of correspondences! He drew up a scheme in various columns. He categorised schoolfriends, primary school teachers, grammar school teachers, university teachers. Superiors and subordinates. Comrades-in-arms (fallen/ missing/ dead and living). Friends/ acquaintances/ neighbours/ relatives/ friends of his parents/ figures from his childhood. Doctors/ fellow students/ literati/ contemporaries. Places of peace/ places of war/ dwelling places/ holiday places/ destinations. Apartments/ barracks/ quarters/ lodgings.

What did Vögele the dentist have to do with Aunt Jenny? Father Kreusler with Gundel Krebs?

Herr Hirschkorn from Silesia with the trumpeter of Freiburg or Klaus Mann?[10]

Volker Aschoff, the schoolboy, with Fräulein Hahn?

Nothing, apart from their presence on his list.

And Martin Raschke, noted under MEN OF LETTERS—what was he, again?

He was neither a comrade-in-arms nor a lodger, so what was he?

Was he a friend, an acquaintance, a destination or a contemporary?

Was he an address, someone to talk to, a memory with the first name Martin?

Was he a colleague, a Saxon, a lyric poet, a prose-writer, a radio author, working-class child, fellow-spirit, corpse, one of the fallen or a victim of the war?

An ethicist specialising in families, a father of daughters, a drinking crony, a travelling companion, a collector of rare stones?

The list had him down as MAN OF LETTERS.

Oh, Babylon!

All the mountains and books were on the list. The sorts of grain, the constellations, the women and the Grand Dukes of Baden.

The continents, the sunflowers and the firms in the Breisgau.

The trees, the breweries and the different sorts of French confectionery.

Stones, stretches of water, illnesses, species of animals and types of ammunition.

The discoverer of Jamaica and the allied commanders.

The whole world and the name of Allah. Allah's name and the whole world.

He himself shoved onto the list—whereabouts?

The list on the list.

Rien ne va plus.[11]

*

On a few occasions, he was able to leave the camp under guard and walk through the vicinity. He went past oases and gardens, saw the Arab farmers' huts, camels and wells. He saw the peaks of the Atlas mountains in the early mornings and the ruined desert forts of the Foreign Legion. He saw a salt lake and was herded further. Once again, he saw the desert and the sand.

*

In April 1947 his release was confirmed.

He was, par excellence, the man for farewells, gifted in broadcasting elegiac sentiments. The sight of the mountains made him melancholy, the desert was good. There was no one to tell him what awaited him back there. Prudence dampened his euphoria—the new freedom could prove bitter. The end of INDIGNITY had arrived; the general sense of relief was great but the farewell among men was not easy for anyone. A firm handshake and a clap on the shoulder propped up the mood sufficiently. A few contacts were maintained, but he never saw the rest of the prisoners again.

The return to Germany lasted several weeks. The transport began through the bureaucratic channels for release. Journey by lorry through the desert and a period of waiting by the sea, jail in Algiers and transport by ship to Marseilles. Shame at the sight of the German depredations in France, continuing his programme of reading and holding farewell conversations. Heart trouble, scepticism, repressed anxiety. Reunion with comrades from anno Elba, memories of better times during the war. Speculating blindly, you stood around in circles, were once again herded together on sports fields, packed tight, stamped and numbered. You were the detested BOCHE in detention. Some prisoners still died, others were transferred into investigative custody as war criminals (you collected bread for them and tried to comfort them). Transport further across France was delayed. Sleepless nights on loading ramps, days on sidings, interrogations, roll calls. A slow train trundling along the banks of the

Rhone, through Lotharingia, Alsace and finally across the Rhine.

The sight of the country in summer numbed the joy. The vineyards and the villages, the tower of the Minster—it was too much to take in. Mixed feelings wrung his insides. The captive cargo went past Freiburg into the Black Forest. Final days in a transit camp, distribution of money, papers and some food; then release towards Freiburg. A man came—nobody was expecting him—to his town. Emaciated, battered and anonymous, he picked his way through a heap of rubble. Past and future stood still; it was the personal moment of no-time and no-thing. Someone or other recognised him on the street (THAT'S DR MECKEL, ISN'T IT? WHERE HAVE YOU COME FROM!). The inculcated manliness suddenly reached its end. It stood there and wept.

V

HYENA PREY, HYENA SELF.
A line from the Fifties, perhaps the bitterest account of his own self, at the least a clear definition of him.

All in all: his most radical statement.

An insight that came like a flash of lightning and would have altered his life, if.

If he could have got a grip on the lightning.

But the sudden illumination was too strong. He was dazzled and could not recognise anything more. Never again did he find himself and a way of defining that self.

*

New start in the French zone. He was thrown back on himself and his weakness. There was no time for heroic attitudes.

The first tram rattled through the rubble, the rest of the town was a pedestrian zone. Grass grew in ruined churches. Squares full of nettles and overcrowded neighbourhoods. Bomb craters and the danger of explosions. Flickering flashlights in dark streets. Dirt tracks and endless treks on foot. The man paralysed by captivity now exhausted his strength running here and there. Permission to go on living was difficult to get. The holy trinity of post war bureaucracy (the labour exchange, the housing bureau and the rations office) had him sitting in their waiting rooms. The occupying authorities had no use for him. An existence lodging overnight in strangers' houses. Searching for old acquaintances and scattered possessions (the books, the clothes, a typewriter). Sleeplessness and strained nerves. He would eat his fill in the kitchens of pre-war friends.

He realised that it was only here in this province that he stood any chance. The name of Meckel was known here. His father and grandfather, architects in Freiburg, had ensured him some public prominence. The tradition of a renowned name provided a basis for his future. He became a freelance contributor to the cultural section of the local paper. Emergency accommodation was secured. It consisted of an attic room and a laundry in the cellar. The attic was pokey, the laundry dank and damp. The house, a hulk from the 1870s, stood among secondary schools and middle-class houses in an intact residential area. The surroundings were agreeable, with gardens, chestnuts, the view onto the mountains and the tolling of nearby bells.

In the summer of 1947, my mother came back from Erfurt to Freiburg, with me, two suitcases and a rucksack. The journey went through three restricted zones and took several days. Arrest at the border of the Russian zone; interrogation in a farm full of refugees; Russians with their mastiffs on chains. Hurried payment of a smuggler, headlong flight out of a back door, past barns and gardens, through the barbed wire, on up the bed of a stream and across the hills. Then, American sentries and no papers. Spending the night on straw on a school staircase (thousands were on the road like us). Waiting in a country railway yard and a long, slow train journey westwards. Whilst my mother kept herself hidden in the railway yard, I sat in sullen helplessness on our luggage and gave evasive answers when checked on. Somehow—always somehow—we kept going. Any particular place was only good for leaving. Slipping past checkpoints, changing trains endlessly, bribing railwaymen, and false papers. In French-occupied Karlsruhe, we were out of danger and a couple of hours later at home in Freiburg.

My brothers were in different zones, installed between the velvet gloves of their grandmothers.

The joyful anticipation of seeing my father was limitless. The memory of early childhood seemed to have gilded the picture of him. I flew to him as if into that gilded image. A few months later, the sheen had disappeared. The disillusion went deep, was confusing at first and then endlessly grey. The demi-god of my child's faith, was a nervous man, an instructor with a need to regain his authority. He worked on re-establishing his family, which meant: on his own controlling position in it. He examined clothes, fingernails and manners, supervised schoolwork and took each ink blot as a reason to make fundamental declarations about work, order, honesty and a child's duty. The first appearance of the declaration: WHAT DO YOU HAVE CHILDREN FOR. A child served any purpose and was forced to perform tasks which, for it, had no point. It swept the graves of its great grandparents and washed crockery in a prescribed order. When tobacco was lacking, it was sent off to fetch cigarettes, while WHAT DO YOU HAVE CHILDREN FOR could be heard, followed by acquiescent laughter.

He was no longer the magician or the friend. He stood like a black cloud between the child and the world, a bitter, tormented and tormenting man-of-precepts who misused the existence of his child to justify himself. His love for me lost any value to me. For the first time I felt sorry for him. He irrevocably and increasingly became a symbol for everything I could not get away from. Whilst still a child, I stopped going to him. Nothing wanted from him and no questions for him. I found what was missing elsewhere. I stole, but I stole nothing from him—not because he was the killjoy overseer but because he had become a stranger who said: I'll give you two Marks and you'll tell me what you used my money for.

He was not well and that was understandable. But his bad health—and only his—darkened every day, and I could not believe that such gloomy days could be my life. He kept going among headaches, exhaustion and permanent irritability. It seemed that his bad health put me in the wrong; it pushed his family—friends and strangers too—into a state of palpitating perplexity. A game evolved where the rules applied as long as FAMILY, his ironclad ideal, supplied the justification for all the efforts and arrangements. The father had come home a changed man; the father was ill and one had to make allowances for him. He was a little helpless, humourless and contradictory—but that would change; he needed time. Making allowances for him became a family illness. It was the reason behind the failure of whatever can be natural and sunny in a mutual attachment. Making allowances for him increasingly came to mean being dishonest towards him. The chronic dishonesty—a burden on your soul—exacerbated the dishonesty of the weakened man towards himself. It denied him any chance of self-awareness. The years staggered along across a subterranean coagulation of things left unsaid. Living together degenerated into a farce, whose sinister paralysis he could not recognise. A frank word in his direction resulted in a heart attack. Heart attacks had to be avoided.

Everyday life post-war happened in the laundry. Whilst rats scurried through the wastepipe, I did my schoolwork at the only table, sat there when visitors came and listened to their conversations. All the visitors were better off than we were. They were my father's friends, some from schooldays; they came from the country and brought things to eat with them. They lived in comparatively affluent circumstances, talked about art and were at home in it. The painters, Dinkelsbühl and Thiel, came, the writer, Egon Vietta and Bartning, the architect.[1] In the evenings, I left the conversations to sleep at someone else's house. There was a bed we could use temporarily. For a year, I slept in strange beds, and that was almost a privilege, despite the inconvenience. To dawdle early and late through the streets, to be able to breathe freely and learn slowly how to observe things, to walk on my own and unsupervised, these things made me happy. For a whole winter, I slept in my relatives' unheated attic. Paula, forty years a general factotum, old, toil-racked, smiling Paula, she put an apple on my bed every evening. The room, the bed, the apples were cold. The apples, the solitude in the cold and reading books I found in the cupboard (tales of knights of old, *Quo Vadis* and *Don Quixote*) all night, this became a dream, which compensated for the absent happiness. The rest was restriction, disappointment and staleness. FAMILY became the everyday burden, and my father became someone who did not count any more.

*

Foraging trips with my father, in summer and autumn days before the currency reform.² War-damaged trains in the black market days. Repaired sleepers, stopping trains, overflowing railbuses on the upper Rhine. Endless treks on foot to sleepy villages. Gaunt war-veteran and gaunt child with empty rucksack on sideroads. Keeping watch at the roadside— and darting like lightning into the farmers' gardens. Cabbages, apples and green tomatoes as booty. Grandiose theft of an unassuming, peacefully growing cauliflower. Proud handful of wrongful beans. Marvellous, always successful smash-and-grab routine.

Better still, to be invited to eat with friends. Out of the laundry, out of the ruined town into spacious, bright houses in the countryside. There was ham, coffee and homemade sausage. Full breadbaskets, full larders and full wine cellars. There was fresh milk for nothing and untallied potatoes. Completely natural orchards full of peaceful pears and innocent nuts, where your stay was pre-approved and free from occupying forces. There was unscathed cider, and wine unsullied by war, well-fed plums and uncompromised bread. There was the luxurious onset of a Gluttons' Peace and there was the first quiet, righteous intoxication. There was the atypical face of a satisfied father, and there was the joy of the child just for that day. There was triumph in the rucksack, kilos of it—the great days of the civilian potato campaigns—and there was the inevitable return to the laundry. There were the tales of daring deeds of free enterprise, and there were the beautiful, too beautiful dreams of escaping the family prison into a Jerusalem full of light, air and chocolate.

*

The house in which he had grown up bordered on the wall of the old cemetery. He had played between the graves; the plane trees and the arcades were a secret Garden of Eden.

Bombs had fallen there during the war. Graves torn open, trees splintered. He collected the fragments of the headstones together, sorting, and numbering before depositing them in a cemetery shed. He did that with care and dedication, as if he were remedying a very personal injury. Nobody had asked him to do it. Before the city engineer took any interest in the graves, he saw to it that nothing went missing. On summer evenings (I watched him, he scraped the rubble away from the bones, and whilst he looked for particular fragments, he recounted the history of the city's families and their names. He showed me the grave of Christian Wenzinger[3] and the grave of an officer from Baden who was said to have been the murderer of Kaspar Hauser.[4] He explained the techniques of masonry to me and what a relief was. Made me aware of the elegiac and solemn memorial art of the baroque.

I have him to thank for what I know about red sandstone.

*

In 1949, a strange bird wandered into the radiance cast by the WHO IS WHO IN GERMANY luminary, Eberhard Meckel. It was Charles Lindbergh[5] on a trip around Europe, an enviably relaxed gentleman from the Happy Far West, and he had come to Freiburg because of my father. Who was E.M. to the American folk-hero? One more star in his diary of notables. All one afternoon, he sat drinking tea in my father's small, book-crammed, badly decorated study, on the bed that doubled as a STUDIO COUCH (the cushions hailed from the time of the currency reform and were sewn together from old curtains), and talked to my parents, which meant using my father's practically non-existent English vocabulary and the half-academic English gained by my mother from her reading of Eliot and Yeats, and all of this in good American faith that here were important Germans. This incursion by world affairs personified into the cramped storey of a housing estate house full of winter coats and creaky floorboards was totally incomprehensible. The affair was odd and so fantastic that it even amused my father. It would have been impossible to declare: we have had a visit from Mister Lindbergh. We recounted the incident as if it were an invention of our own and said: we're expecting the Emperor of China next.

*

From 1949 until his death, he lived on one floor of a housing estate house in the district of Herdern (in order to secure a residence permit and a lease, he had helped to build it for weeks on end). The first year was a good time. Furniture and books were collected together; all our heads under one roof. A volume of collected poems appeared in the Inselverlag. Nothing stopped him working for the radio and the newspapers. He had established himself and his family in a durable framework. It remained the same until his death.

For his children, it meant the end of happiness. They were put into a small room. The smallness of the room suited the father's wishes: he could oversee the closely contained happenings. Every day he sat at his desk (with his feet in a fur-lined box on cold days, EXTRA HEATING from the post-war times) and tapped out bread-and-butter articles on the typewriter. I would watch him, sitting at that desk, writing and thinking. His thought process was ponderous; he lacked the light touch, sparkle and, above all, humour. I was bewildered by the sight of a man sitting there who was never sovereign over his own powers. I saw a worker with no detachment from his work and wondered at this heavy labourer pouring out his strength reliably, punctually and for miserable wages. He lived beyond his powers to no small extent; he toiled with every fibre for his family. And his fibre was extraordinarily resilient despite his exhausted nerves. I thought to myself: a poor devil and was ashamed, and yet I knew: he had willed that toil. Without toil, there was no life for him; he needed toil as the light touch was denied him. No wings, but shoes of lead. Without them, he would have dissolved into melancholia or been eaten up with scruples and worries. His hackwork, felt to be DRUDGERY, was the one sure way not to go under.

He perched there, shrouded in contemplation, brooding nervously, sounding out half-formed sentences, listening, as it were, for his own thoughts, mulling over a theme. Thinking without writing was not his way; he needed a text as a basis for his thoughts. Diderot's thinking occurred in a dialogue and out loud, a constant stream of verbal extraversion. Leopardi's thinking was a tragic monologue. Stendhal dictated the *Chartreuse de Palme* in seven weeks, transposing his already composed text. Flaubert wrote *Madame Bovary* in five years, dragging his prose together, word by word, thinking in exploratory sentences and noting down language in order to manage any thinking at all.[6] My father belonged to the class of BRAINWORKERS who thought ponderously, slowly categorising things. Thinking meant hard work for him.

He was a good reviewer, and would have been a better one if he had been able to conceive of criticism not as paid work but as literature. Criticism (in the sphere of literature and art) seemed his strongest gift— involvement with things outside of him distracted him from himself. An aesthetic eclecticism and empathy, the cultivated and critical recapitulation of existing work, that was a branch he underestimated. He saw himself as POET and suffered under his profession. He wrote a few hundred reviews, newspaper articles and feuilletons (the hard-earned PETTY CASH). He discussed recently published literature, yearbooks of art-history and the almanacs produced in Baden. He reviewed theatre premières, chamber pieces and films, wrote about musicals, Beckett and Thornton Wilder, Shakespeare and the one-night wonders of the previous season, about amateur performances in the provinces and student theatre. He produced articles about wine tastings, grand openings, Black Forest spas and Hebel anniversaries in the Wiesental. About readings in the town library and art-exhibitions in the region. His almost incessant SCRIBBLING generated something like a local catalogue of the cultural events after the currency reform. The cultural policy of the occupying authorities was progressive. Very early after the war, institutes sprang up in which concerts and speeches could be heard. The enlightened world broke in on unenlightened Freiburg. You orientated yourself towards Paris and Zurich—existentialism and chocolate. Sartre, Camus[7] and the "isms" of the Forties became the ideas recapitulated in discussions everywhere. The cellar-theatre, the municipal theatre and the Society of Arts, the Conservatory of Music and the university underpinned the reconstruction of the epoch in that sleepy wine country. Beckett, Orff or Dallapiccola,[8] only just becoming public, were brought to Freiburg. The first schoolbooks for teaching German were the best there ever were in Germany. World literature (selected according to French criteria), chansons, social criticism and human rights, an emancipation of the most uncomfortable kind was too much for the grammar school teachers (they had been in the Party and now found it difficult to cut credible figures). For the first time I read Heine, Herwegh and Lessing, Engels, Voltaire, Diderot[9] and REVOLUTION. In the corridors of the CASINO, between blocked-off ballrooms, I saw the first exhibitions after the war, Picasso, Beckmann, Camaro, Masson and the new abstracts from the Ecole de Paris.[10] All that was contradictory, exciting, new—and overwhelming for a child who had come out of the Russian zone undernourished and ignorant.

As a journalist firmly encased in solid sensibility, my father followed all that. It left no discernible trace on him and on what he wrote. I have rarely seen a talented person as incapable of change as he was. He held popular courses at the adult education centre, introducing people to literature. He visited the artists in their studios, observed their work and supported them. They had him to thank for inspiration, promotion of their names in the press and for practical criticism (he similarly supported actors). He took part in journalists' conferences, travelled to book fairs, participated in cultural debates locally and, as a journalist, became known throughout the town.

*

The writer remained, in what he did produce, behind all the literary advances of the post-war years. He did not seem interested in new contacts, although they were open to him as a reviewer. He still visited Horst Lange and Günter Eich, was himself visited by Goes and Huchel; they sent each other their new publications, but all that had no effect on him. Neither side resurrected the friendships of the Thirties. His faith in his own language disappeared; the daily hackwork consumed his powers. He continued his research into Hebel, was one of the first to produce interpretations shifting the domesticated creator of the Alemannic language out of parochial belittlement and into classical literature (his best prose was a text on Hebel). A selection of his own poetry, his last book, appeared in the Aufbauverlag in the GDR. That made him enemies in conservative Baden and reinforced him in his belief that he was an author of some consequence. But overall—and increasingly so—he restricted himself to existing acquaintances in the provinces. Here existed a loose grouping of aesthete authors, the FREIBURG CIRCLE, founded and led by him, They were feuilleton writers and literary medical men, locally significant names like Franz Schneller, Ernst Sander, the Balzac translator, and Heinrich Weis. Among them, Kurt Heynicke,[11] white-haired, old. He counted as the last living Expressionist (once the youngest author in the MENSCHHEITSDAMMERUNG),[12] had compromised his writing during the Third Reich with popular novels and had grown bitter in his long resignation. (I visited the old man in his village, he sat stooped over his kitchen table, vigorous and sour, a man without any great successes, who wrote his best poetry in his old age and was livelier than the downcast curl of his lips averred). They met in apartments or inns, mistreated each other, became enemies, became reconciled and discussed the new trends from the local perspective. Various gentlemen spoke out against these, showed their animosity to contemporaries and rejected political influences. A curious club with high-minded interests and, nolens volens, a world to itself.

*

In Freiburg there lived, floated and faded a sort of benevolent local spirit.

He was called Toni Müller and was an old man. He had gone to Prague before the First World War, had got to know Kafka and Werfel[13] there, published a volume of poetry INADVERTENTLY, then whiled away the war in a government office making a hash of call-up lists. He had come to rest later on in Freiburg. As a columnist on the local paper, writing under a pseudonym, he made his living from a few lines, a whole column each weekend (what colleagues paid for a meal lasted the Prince of Pocket Money for ten days). He wrote small feuilletons, glossaries of Alemannic language in the tone of a charming gossip, explained the origins of Alemannic words, their old and new meanings and their use, a semanticist without a title or a degree, an unselfish custodian of scholarship.

Like a peaceful old dog he trotted, always alone, through the beautiful town, poor but clean, a sprite in a beret. He was a lodger somewhere (no-one seemed ever to have entered his den), overflowed with affability and had no enemies. Isolation seemed to have made him seek refuge in limitless acquiescence. Always smiling, smiling no matter what, he went smiling through the neighbourhood, scattering anecdotes (always the same) and became a saint without a halo or a blemish. This unarmed individual disarmed everyone. I was glad to be disarmed and to sit with him over a glass of wine and listen to the same stories over and over again. Stories wrapped in overflowing, silent laughter. Anecdotes told to avoid talking about himself. Anecdotes—a discreet way of dancing on tear-bottles[14] and not spilling a drop. A very deliberately restricted life, in which the old Wandering Jew came to light, in the guise of a stroller though the Black Forest metropolis. He had decided to find himself funny, presumably the only chance of not perishing. And so he lived somehow and died sometime, a DELECTABLE MOUNTAIN, who did no one any harm.

I propose a place in Paradise for him, that is: in the INTERNATIONAL OF GOOD PEOPLE founded by Gedalje and Isaac Babel.[15]

*

His conscience was stricken. The question of German guilt would not leave him in peace. It could only be answered by surrendering the personal probity he affirmed so strongly. But he did not surrender his probity.

He hoped to survive the bout by a win on points.

What he said gave no insight into what he had done in the Nazi period and into what he had thought. His role in the larger context did not become clear. His accounts remained anecdotal: the horrors of war—YOU HAVE NO IDEA! We had no idea and believed him. He declared his disgust at the German crimes, and there were a couple of obscure points in what he said. He did not seem sure of his righteous indignation. His personal sense of guilt and the repression of it—his life depended increasingly on repressions—kept his conscious intellect hard at work every day.

Now he did nothing that was not good and proper. He did it out of a sense of citizen's responsibility and he did it to appease his conscience. He donated money to worldwide appeals, for humane, social and political purposes. He supported the local SPD.[16] He appeared at community meetings, opposed the Emergency Laws,[17] made himself conspicuous by his critical stance in public discussions—and that was as it should be. It was DECENT, as he himself said. It was not possible to avoid doing the right thing now, and he did the right thing with a vengeance. He was just too much wrapped up in it and there was just too much talk of it. A strange and restless assertiveness dogged the propriety of what he did. He had burdens to work off. He was gathering points.

His war stories would end with the claim that he had at all times BEHAVED IMPECCABLY, that he had—for example—contradicted his superiors, that he had spoken up for other people and often prevented the very worst. He recounted the same incident several times. A recollection of a military transport through occupied Poland. The train stopped near a village; you packed the windows and looked out into the Steppes. Women and children stood begging by the tracks and endured the soldiers' jokes. My father threw a piece of bread (A BIG CHUNK) into the hands of a young Polish woman. She thanked him tearfully and ran off to the village.

He said: that was really quite decent of me. I didn't need to do that.

I often heard similar stories. My youth was full of his good deeds, and I was convinced I had an unimpeachable father. Later, I recognised the connection: the original spontaneity of his reaction had meanwhile become worth a few extra points for him. The subsequent upgrading of a spontaneous gesture into the good deed done by a German angered me. He seemed to believe that working off guilt like this had some sort of meaning. Few things made me feel so wretched as did his murky conscience's strategy of winning on points.

I listened to people who told me I was wrong. Ex-soldiers made it clear to me that the good deed (the bread given) demanded civil courage in those days. Under the prevailing circumstances (GERMAN OCCUPATION IN ENEMY POLAND), he could possibly have been punished for such an act; in any case, it was not without risk. Whoever gave a piece of bread (which apparently did not happen very often) drew undesirable attention to himself. He was in danger of being denounced by his comrades (they themselves had nothing to eat). I hear these sentences with a feeling of vertigo, do not know any better and do not want to be in the right. But the crediting of him with the bread depresses me. Being set straight about the incident does not make me happy.

The wish for memories that do not exist and the wish for conversations that never took place. The notion of finding poems by him (in a drawer, underneath tax returns) that could eclipse his existence.

*

Not much about him existed as a matter of course. The capacity for improvising was missing, for forgetting himself and for nonchalance. EASYGOING, REALLY EASYGOING was a frequent saying, and CHEERFUL, UTTERLY CHEERFUL his unrealisable wish. Whatever he said—he emphasised it. Whatever he did—he drew attention to it. The deficient basis of his personality, in constant stress, needed the confirmation of himself as an individual. His self-confidence, disturbed from childhood on, had fallen apart after the war and was forcibly—every day afresh—reinstated at the expense of his family.

Because he could no longer appear as governor of his people; as the patriarchal role became increasingly unbelievable; as his need to be the boss—always unsuccessful and from the very beginning anachronistic—did not earn gratitude but rejection; as he could be only the head of the family, the decision-making man of the house (there was no helping him); as he played the role from top to bottom without realising that it was not the family that needed him but he the family and its obedience; as he never gained any insight into himself, he took refuge in a series of substitutes. He decked himself out with all available illusions for the rest of his life. To remain immovably the same, he mobilised a new identity and established it through proverbs, maxims and quotations. He had to preserve himself as the core of the family, although he was only its shattered husk. Let it cost what it would, and it did cost everything. His wife's strength exhausted itself in the attempt to making living and co-existence bearable.

He made himself into the benefactor of his family. The governor tried being a partner and a friend. Each one of us was individually fitted into his attempt at a new concept of his role. What was, over and over again, meant to be simply family was subjected to his new style of self-assertiveness. The friendship was embarrassing, the sympathy irksome; just breathing freely every day was smothered by a saccharine compulsion. What he could not achieve by rules and regulations (to dominate and to be loved), he achieved by kindness, at whatever price. The velvet glove of this Saturn made itself felt, and it, so he thought, had a grip on the situation. He drove his people to wherever they wanted to go: to railway stations, parties, concerts and schools, to holiday resorts, all sorts of appointments—and he picked them up again. He put his car, library and wine cellar at their disposal. He helped with the housework and tried to please everyone. He found his way into their lives through a thousand cunningly opened backdoors. He courted them with help and gifts, sent them parcels they did not want, bought books they did not need, clothes and shoes they no longer lacked. He visited them wherever they were, but only to throw out his lasso again. His kindness succeeded in putting them in the wrong. The gratitude of his people was a long time coming. He uttered his complaints and noted them down: fulfilling the wishes of his children wore him down; the endless demands such egotists made. There were no demands on him and no wishes of him. He ostentatiously stuffed twenty-mark notes into their jacket pockets, noted the sums and later declared: he had spent three hundred Marks in two years, but that did not matter, it was not a question of debts, he was only saying.

A man's blind devaluation of himself. His brokenness tormented his children (they did not know that this father role—the dethroned despot now grown helpless—was typical of a whole generation). Their protest was all the more difficult because he did love them.

Bewilderment over many years. Trepidation. There was never any fresh air; laughter faded out. The children could not yet cope with their father's psychic dilemma. They had no patience with him; they had, above all, no time. They sought a fatherless life for themselves; they demanded happiness and needed the whole world. When they did come to understand, there was still time. He perished amid the forbearance of those who knew him.

*

He had spent his holidays in Tirol and came back home with a votive painting.

The painting came from a chapel in the mountains. He had discovered it in the sacristy and taken it with him because it was neglected. It was over a hundred years old, oils on a small cherry-wood board, and depicted an accident. A farmer had wound up under his wagon. He lay with crushed legs under a dray loaded with tree trunks. In the background a road ran away; honest-faced, fat horses were standing there and a few pines with cones that looked like strawberries. Above it all sat the Madonna in her cloud, a flutter of crudely painted scrolls with petitions around her, while she looked with grey eyes in no particular direction.

He unwrapped the picture from out of a few cloths and presented it: MY DISCOVERY!

Then he got himself some oil paints, brushes and turpentine. Although he had bread-and-butter work to finish, he sat for days at his desk, cleaned the frame and filled the wormholes with colourless paste. He painted over the beautiful crazed surfaces, traced over grey contours with black paint and buried the natural patina under make-up. He had never restored a picture, his dilettantism was ruinous, but that did not bother him; his pleasure outweighed it. That all happened with the intention of keeping the picture. It became a topic in the family.

Had he stolen the picture?

There can be no question of theft. He has not stolen the picture but has rescued it. You might say that he has borrowed it; that the chapel is the wrong place for it; that it is exposed to the weather there and not safe from thieves, will inevitably be damaged; the chapel is old, the lock on the door smashed; that in his room, it is secure, although he doesn't regard it as his property; that he regards it as a loan—well, a loan for an indefinite period.

So he'll take it back to the chapel?

We'll see.

We said: of course he'll take back the picture. You can't expect anything else. As a Catholic he is obliged to restore the picture and then give it back. It hung for a year in my father's room. We asked repeatedly what is going to happen with the picture, and he gave evasive answers. The picture belongs to the person who rescues it and cares for it. The game was malicious and he did not notice. We wanted him to have the picture (we liked it a lot), but we also wanted to know if he could be moved to return it. He was not a hardened church-robber. Although he had not intended to spend his holidays in Tirol, he went there and took the picture back to the chapel.

*

Once the cat was out of the house, the mice would dance on the table. Music at full volume and open doors, friends and girl friends, uproar in the night.

Unordained, glorious fun.

Or else peace, profound peace. Unlimited, fatherless peace.

*

He seemed to be notable in many people's eyes, and whoever did not experience his weakened state was glad to see him. Outside of the family and the WORKADAY (and in as far as his obsessions did not turn destructive), as critic at exhibition openings, in an inn after theatre premières, he presented himself as an intact personality. He had studied art-history in Munich with Wölfflin and German with Kutscher,[18] was an unacademic Ph.D. with the airy, aesthetic aura of a man of letters, a notable person who stressed his own worth. His acquaintances were numerous, his friendships old: professors and editors, actors, doctors and businessmen from the province. All that had the appearance of a well-founded life and would have been unassailable if it had been lived amid the free play of his powers.

*

Divining-rod prose.

The divining-rod jerks with every memory of things embarrassing, dubious and terrible.

It jerks at the thought of all that was good. Of everything indubitable about the man.

*

I would like to have known him as a more accessible personality, at least a little more accessible and very much more free and easy. I would like to invent tall tales for his benefit, very much like to fake things and weave spells for him.

I am loathe to have his weaknesses weighing upon him, his state of mortal debilitation and his life as a losing bargain. I am loathe to see him saddled with my criticism. In desperation, memory seeks his being, latches onto something and makes prose out of it.

*

Whenever the children came home from friends, holidays and their first loves, from whole epochs spent in light and carelessness, whole eras full of snow

whenever they stood worn out at the door into the garden with bicycles, rucksacks, bruises and sunburn

whenever they came home with torn trousers, with small debts or a bit late, with ruined shoes and dirty paws

whenever they raced hot-headed through the apartment, full of fantastic tales and showed enthusiasm (a fearful mistake)

whenever it turned out that they were happy, outside of the house, in the wide world, at parties and on the roam, beyond their father

whenever they filled out the narrow, unchanging apartment with everything that they were (not disguising it quickly enough)—

then the magic was all over inside of an hour. The father ran the bathwater.

There followed the thorough removal of all foreign matter: the dust on their legs and the unconcealed joy, the sweat in their hair and the unfettered experience, the happiness without their parents, without supervision and duty. The children had had their holidays; now their schoolbags were cleaned out. An hour later they appeared in the usual mould: creatures of the family. The noisy vigour was stilled; the usual mildew settled over their dreams. The father was content with the appearance of peace. He had used the absence of the children to clean out their cupboards.

Everything in order.

*

Everything that was lacking from childhood and youth. All the lacking things in total.

Early on, the awareness developed, pervasive and incomprehensible, of a huge lack.

Space was lacking in all respects. Living-space, rooms and open passages were lacking. Nooks and crannies and your own little hideaway were lacking. Tables, chairs, toys, radios and sideboards were lacking, the pointless, lovely and luxurious things were lacking. Free wall-space was lacking and hence the pictures too; the cupboard for a modest secret was lacking; your own room with a lock on it was lacking, and hence singing, running, dreaming and elation too. Play fell silent; dawdling vanished, being absent, taking yourself off, spending a night alone. The wealth of rich people is their money, but more so in the space and the prodigality with room, much more so in unrestricted mobility. The father was worried, a frugal man, and the bread in the family's breadbaskets was sparse. The children hailed from a background that did not exist: starvelings from the intellectual proletariat. They were worse dressed than other school children, fed more meagrely, and their home was more nightmarish. The youngest child wore out the trousers of the older ones; a rich uncle sent used clothes. What is really fine is a house with rooms to spare; what is really superb are unused nooks, cellars, sheds, storerooms and verandas, maids' rooms, guestrooms, bathrooms, larders, stairways and attics. What is enviable and fine are old wardrobes, roomy toilets and open balconies. In my grandparents' house, there was a dressing-room; my father's apartment had less than what we needed. The restriction became a nightmare, something unavoidable. Space was measured out to the smallest fraction, tell-tale walls and rooms like cells—everything was lacking, but that was not the worst. Childhood was lived out in allocated space; that was a misery shared by many and was not the worst.

Joy was lacking, luxury and happiness.

Happiness was lacking for many, but not for everyone. The absence of joy was common to many people, but not to all. The lack of joy—a result of the war—was an affliction shared by many, but not by all. The absence of joy in my father's family was the result of a fundamental *mauvaise foi.*[19]

The war had ruined families. Fathers staggered back home, got to know their children and were rejected as impostors. Initially they were exhausted and had not a good word for anyone. The place kept free for fathers was taken over by strangers, who were foreign and hostile, or wrecks, and who adopted the posture of parents—that was not credible. Damaged marriages and disturbed emotions, ruins, hunger and bad prospects for the future, socks darned ten times over and cold stoves—how could there be joy in those families. Happiness had been something secure the day before yesterday, for the future it was not certain, and a LUXURY—what else could it be at a time when people were snatching after hope, the hope of being able to breathe freely.

It was not a matter of pastries and silks but of joy and its absence.

The German family in the no-longer-German Land of Four Zones was busy with repression, with war neuroses and with placating guilt, with ruined nerves and impotence. It was busy with the results of anxiety and confusion; it grew sick from intellectual exhaustion and wore itself out with depression. A whole generation seemed to be busy licking wounds, deserved and undeserved. The majority of the Germans were patching up spiritual and material holes. You rummaged around, anxiously and hectically and for who knows how long, in a private or collective identity now grown threadbare, and found no confirmation of anything any more. I, you and we stood perplexed amid a guilt known worldwide, wanted peace and quiet and retreated into the womb of the family. In those days, you craved a good conscience and buried the bad one under potato peelings. Instead of straight answers to straight questions, a great effort at extenuation took hold everywhere. It resounded and sighed in all families, falsified its own echo and granted itself its own pardon. It was capable of any exoneration. It was the rotten heart in the body of Germany.[20] What was called the reconstruction of the state and the family quickly and piously revealed itself as an act of restoration. You sought new straws for the old nest. You were somebody again if you could feed your wife and children.

In all that, where was joy supposed to come from.

It was lacking.

It was lacking in my father more than in others, and it was denied to his children more than to others.

Every little extra was lacking.

It was not the extras you missed but a diversity in the father's personality and openness in the everyday life of the family. As everything was apportioned and accounted for, the unallotted residue, the surplus was lacking. Happy unpredictability was lacking, the improvised party and smacking your lips and slurping over a ripe pear. Anything marvellous was lacking even at the best times; the lack seemed to have no beginning and never came to an end.

Joy was lacking.

Although the father was capable of joy, could be happy sometimes, really happy, his joy remained a small thing; it did not carry over. It was no wildly spendthrift paradise; it did not shine or strew blossoms; it did not make the children as happy as it did him and did not bring any pure and simple pleasure for each of us.

Great, all-embracing joy was not there. It was lacking each day, each night, on all occasions, at all times. It was already gone before waking and was still lacking long after sleep had come. The chance to breathe and dream free of restrictions was lacking; the unselfconscious tenderness was lacking. Spontaneous elation for no good reason. Or for a good and exciting reason. Unconsidered words were lacking and light-hearted conversations, nonchalance, tolerance and frivolity were lacking. A stock of sympathy for the father was lacking; a laisser-faire attitude towards the failings of his children; limitless forgiveness was lacking and, in consequence, love.

Acoustic and optical sensations were lacking; the sensual excitement of things beyond the everyday, prodigal bouquets, clothes, music, the sparkling colours and the steaming dishes were lacking. Room for anger and boundless laughter was lacking—but gloom enough existed to fill all the rooms. Duty was there (WHY DO YOU HAVE CHILDREN ANYWAY), enforced quietness, studied harmoniousness.

Unrealized anger and unrealized joy. They packed up and went elsewhere. They wandered through the world and remained themselves, jog-on, jog-on, wandering through the world. They had come into the world in a child and did not know the taste of adulthood yet.

Jog-on, jog-on.

The father's joy was not popular with the children. What was their instructor's joy worth to them, anyway. His laughter showed that he could still laugh, and a family party showed that he knew how to celebrate with his people.

Always the lack. Always the lack.

Glasses smashed against the wall were lacking. You do not have to hurl wine glasses at the wall. It is not desirable and does not have to happen. Millions of people have never hurled wine glasses at the wall and despite that have not missed out on any anger and joy.

But: it was not allowed. And so: it was lacking.

The marks down the wall of some calamity and the broken glass on the carpet were lacking, but the dustpan was not lacking. The dustpan was never lacking; never the brush either. Never the floorcloth; never the command to clean up. The freedom from the father was lacking; it was lacking and lacking. Spills, breakages and things bubbling over were lacking. A thoroughgoing prodigality was lacking, but the mildew, the mildew was always there.

It coated the whole family with dullness. The father's name was mildew; the childhood illness was mildew. Mildew, mildew. Mildew was never lacking.

Where were families in which you could live like a human being? Where could you embrace and laugh by an open window? Where could you play, sing and make music without any ulterior purpose, permission, appointed time and good reason? Where did those people live who giggled companionably, strewed salt in the beds and wore false noses to their meals. Where was the kingly laughter that made allotting roles absurd? Where was the laughter that made careworn faces beautiful?

Always the lack. Always the lack.

Embracing, self-irony and clear thinking were lacking. The open stream of vigorous life was lacking. Confetti clouds of divine nonsense were lacking and the smallest twitch of arbitrariness. The careless waste of time was lacking, and so any spare time at all was lacking. The physical freedom between parents and children was lacking; the open words and open doors were lacking. Pleasure in nakedness or laughter over it were lacking.

The pitiful lack cried to Heaven and God's mercy.

In everything and for everything, a true word was lacking. Genuine contradiction was lacking because the father was lacking who would entertain contradictions. Mockery and rebellion were not lacking; there was no lack of joy found elsewhere—it was just that, in the family jail, simple fresh air was lacking.

A bottle of wine, drunk at night, still had its use beyond intoxication; it brought a shared or solitary sense of relief; it let you forget all the wretchedness; it meant a precarious, makeshift and temporary truce with the promoter of a home-grown *mauvaise foi*.

The wine that tasted good was drunk elsewhere.

Jog-on, jog-on.

What signified openness and could have been real life, that was all submerged in the father's brooding. What stood for insight, argument and conviction foundered over his refusal to correct himself. The answer to a question about his role in the war foundered over his refusal to speak plainly. Insight foundered amid repression. The golden thread was lacking in his weave.

Always the lack. Always the lack.

The acceptance of the children's' unwashed necks was lacking as was the acceptance of thoughts alien to the father. Neither Goethe's nor Schiller's poems were lacking, but the acknowledgement of interests not already contained within the family was lacking. What the father promoted was a constant devaluation, the devaluation of himself and of the others' lives.

He was the devaluer.

Life was elsewhere.

*

A child had no chance to be rid of him.

He leapt onto the backs of his children and cried: you feed your old father, you owe him something!

The children disappeared in apathy and dreams, in a creeping or a volcanic depression. They were of no use in the bourgeois world. For days and nights on end, they wandered around, played truant and came home too late. They played dead in the father's sphere of authority, said nothing, in their apathy, rebellion or arrogance. They hung around in school without achieving anything. They wished their father dead and attacked him, took every chance to get out and sought life where they could find it. Anywhere else had more of it than here.

Their spiritual misery was enormous. The father's order-loving eye noticed nothing. They were on the verge of becoming criminal and were seen with dubious types at the railway station. They scoured the parking grounds with car thieves, plundered slot machines, broke into houses and stole money. One disappeared, aged ten, and was picked up abroad. The other roamed around with suicide on his mind. Revolt and destruction were their daily bread, and their nightly bread, their only bread.

There was only perishing or becoming stronger. Laughter still had to be learned, elsewhere.

VI

My father wanted successful sons in the framework of bourgeois ideas about respectability and a secure income. He formulated his wishes to them in poetry: to go on dreaming the work he created to its end. Those were the pious wishes of a poet; the proposals of the bourgeois father looked more practical.

I intended to become an architect. People agreed that I had talent, an extraordinarily developed SENSE OF SPACE (whatever that was), the technical knowledge and social interests. It was decreed that I should finish technical school, then study architecture and be successful as a freelance architect. He supported this proposal and approved of it. Architecture belonged to his homeground, in the realm of art and family tradition, and was at the same time removed from his own position. For years, I conformed innocently to his concept of my life.

Then my interests and commitment changed. I began to draw and to write poems. That was a matter allowing no compromise. I plunged into it, and there was no more to be said. School was neglected. The family cage lost its terrors. Drawing and writing, I left them behind me. That I did drawings was quite in order; drawing counted as one of an architect's skills and could only be to my advantage later. Writing poetry, that was a different question.

When I was away on holiday, my father had, found quite a few sheets of lyric poetry in my schoolbag (he was in the habit of inspecting his children's junk). I was not yet fifteen years old. He had me come to his room that evening. The formality of the summons signalled impending torment. Like a boss, busy with papers, he sat at his desk and requested me to sit down. The ridiculousness of the ritual was crushingly effective, although I knew it of old. His face wore an expression of sombre, considered seriousness. He was determined to put me in the wrong.

So you write poems?

I said yes.

In his extreme irritation, he declared: don't get any ideas, your verse is bad. Everybody writes poems at some time or other, it's just a phase. Don't imagine you have any talent, you haven't. Your field is architecture. I can't forbid you to write poetry, but I do advise you to give it up.

I shouted that writing was my business and stormed out of his performance.

From that day on, he was uneasy. A monster as yet unidentified had broken into his reserve. He did not know how to deal with it and would have liked to render it a little bit extinct. Pointed remarks had no effect on it; outbursts of rage tried to bury it. (You are nothing, you are capable of nothing, do your homework!) I was amazed, then worried and finally immune when I noticed the man's helplessness.

His unease increased when he found out that his poetry said nothing to me. It became excessive when he realised that my case could not be closed.

I wrote flashy, bad poetry, stormy lyric, bellowing bombast, copied Rimbaud[1] and thundered through all the forms. He seemed to convince himself—successfully—that this behaviour did not mean anything. There was no more talk of it for months; he seemed to have calmed down and said nothing. My interest in art was as well received as ever; the writing of poetry was embargoed.

I did not let on anything about myself or my affairs. The man and what he thought and wanted were no longer important to me. I saw my life open up and rushed into it. Silence surrounded his monopoly: language. He made me feel that I was stupid.

A few years later, I was studying graphic art in Munich. My first poems were published there in 1955. My father's commentary from a distance: perhaps talented, but don't get any ideas. I did not get any ideas, but wrote poems. The critical responses, public and private, caused him to keep his attacks within limits. I could see: he would rather have added his voice to a condemnation. Then books came, and they wounded him. The monster in his reserve was expanding. It took over the whole space and, in its cruel innocence, pushed the previous owner up against the wall. Additional sufferings then set in for a man who was already profoundly weakened anyway. I went on with my life self-righteously and did not notice a thing. The pious and practical wishes were finished. Whatever I did went beyond him into a life that he did not know. He was weakening, and I did not notice. His sense of self, anchored to a set of ideals and shored up by received ideas, once again collapsed amid crises. As a lyric poet, he lost his position in the chaos of a disintegrating identity. He could do nothing to change it and nothing to help himself. He resigned and came over to my side in a long, painful process, where doubt, love and envy merged. He let it be known, with passable good humour, that he had become the father of his son.

YOU WRITE THE POEMS THAT I WANTED TO WRITE.

The mere fact of my existence rendered his hollow. Whatever I wrote made him all the poorer. I could see: he was suffering because he was overshadowed by me; he was suffering because of his son and was proud of him. He found no authentic happiness in this conflict. He took refuge in unconditional affirmation. It did not blind him to my weaknesses nor did it disarm his critical ability—he was simply discouraged and felt he had been sidelined. I did not want that and could do nothing for him. His affirmation did not make me happy. What could have flattered me oppressed me instead. His drive to produce was sorely weakened. The illusion transferred itself to the private sphere. What had been denied to him as a POET, he had achieved as a man and a father. He had made his family happy and had fed them through his work.

Now he sought solace from the person who had made him disconsolate. He set great store by conversations and became the friend who promoted the work of the other. His friendship surrounded me and did not let go; I tried to loosen it by being amiable. It was an ambiguous strategy and the only possibility to let him go on living. He was the self-appointed, staunch friend and lived off the fact that I wrote the poems. He lived off the amiability of his sons, and more so, off the amiability of his wife. He lived for a long time off considerate treatment. The considerateness prolonged his agony.

He would increasingly talk about my poems as if he had written them himself.

A reading was proposed for an opening of an exhibition of my graphics. I was not able to be there and cancelled it; my father went. He felt called on to appear, without my knowledge, and to read my poems. He read the poems in a way that made people think they were his own.

As he was dying, he still lived, as POET, off thoughts of me and my poems.

*

A saddening diminution of life. I watched my father becoming less and less by the year. Daily work became TINKERING and writing SCRIBBLING. In this limited state, he found a measure of stability. As a critic and journalist he was confronted by all the literary, philosophical, ideological and scientific trends of the time, but he only seemed to register them for professional purposes, with a view to the next newspaper article. A fundamental renunciation seemed to alienate him from himself. He did seem to take note of contemporary events, and as far as poetry went, his curiosity remained active, but nothing of what he read or heard impelled him to produce something of his own. He became increasingly lonely through a lack of inner flexibility. The attempt to write a novel failed. After twenty sides, he gave up the effort. At first he said in his usual grand manner: we will, in fact, have to see if he had a proper idea of his readership. But he had no readership and neither the strength internally nor the time externally. In as far as he did write for himself, he produced a feature writer's prose and complained that he could not find a publisher for it.

He did one time declare confidently that over the years a few things had, in fact, collected in drawers. I still believed the tone of self-confidence, suggested that he send me the manuscripts and promised to interest a few publishers in them. From that moment, the tone ceased. The manuscripts did not arrive. I asked him again over the phone; at that, he snapped that there was time yet and that he had no wish to be pushed and put under an obligation. After a few weeks the manuscripts were there: about twenty newspaper clippings stuck onto paper. All in all, that did not amount to much. They turned out to be philosophical and agreeable, rather old-world observations, not to be compared with literary prose. I wanted to keep my promise, sent the manuscript to a publisher and got it back. The rejection, to which I was already resigned, was a low blow and destroyed what was left of his illusions. They were restored once again by a local prize for literature, but his self-confidence had been destroyed. The manuscript disappeared into his desk and was never mentioned again. In his despair, he did not believe that he counted any more. He declared he had no right to call himself a writer. He quoted Hölderlin: ICH BIN NICHTS MEHR, ICH LEBE NICHT MEHR GERNE. (I am nothing any more; I am no longer glad to be alive). What I said to him about it could not help him. My intervention on his behalf actually did him a bad turn. I blamed myself. It would have been better to avoid making the broken man confront himself. The illusion of being unrecognised would have sustained him; the chronic bitterness would have borne him up in the end. He could only maintain his self-image through self-deception. I saw his face drawn with dismay and did not find it easy to cope with my regret.

*

He drew attention to himself: he laid great emphasis on his own merits. If a token of recognition found its way into the house (the writer did not often find himself honoured), it was gilded to last as long as possible. His modesty irritated me. SCRIBBLING instead of writing—how did you do that? How did he manage to write poems without going beyond his limits? What sort of man was it who booked LAUDATORY MENTIONS to his own credit? What was wrong with him that he could regard the public illumination of his name as something crucial? How shamefully easy it was to satisfy the man. A question directed to him as an authority—and he would wax large with wide-ranging answers. A word of acknowledgement for his work—and he showed the most fawning complaisance. It took a while until I realised why, and yet it was difficult to excuse my secret pity for him.

The abiding concern coming up to his sixtieth birthday revolved around the question: what could we expect? Would anything happen at all? Would his friends and enemies remember him? Would the press publish a few congratulatory articles? This date was the last chance to draw public attention to him, wasn't it?

He was glad that something actually happened. Grateful. Moved. Flowers, visitors and telephone calls, gestures from the town's cultural committee and telegrams of congratulation from various ministries, all that was a relief to him beyond measure. The man-with-a-birthday put on a jovial face. And when he received an academy's honorary award, he opened the best wine and declared repeatedly: children, you don't know what a father you've got!

*

In 1960, Emil Strauss died in an old people's home in Freiburg. He was ninety-four. You could see him under the trees on the Karlsplatz, a limping figure with a walking stick, the left-over debris of a self-confident misanthrope. My father sometimes met him on the street. He was waiting for death, said Strauss, he had had enough.

Emil Strauss was considered a significant prose-writer next to Hauptmann, Stehr[2] and Thomas Mann and was famous in the decades before the Second World War. The old man had become a Nazi and, with that, a state-approved, classic author of the Thirties. There was much talk of his inward decline. In Josef Nadler's history of literature[3] he had been hailed as an Alemannic writer ("Close to Hebel's poems, which he published tastefully, this dignified, sensually tasteful, reserved and austere man, his noble prose inspired by dialect, is the embodiment of this landscape and its spiritual influences from the Latin world".) The fact that Strauss lived in Freiburg seemed to concern my father more than the fact that the respected narrator had been a Nazi.

On the day of the funeral he noted:

> "In the morning the cremation of Emil Strauss. At the close, after fine words from Father K. and wreaths from Pforzheim, University, Goethe Foundation, State Government, the town and the Hanser Verlag, I said this: writers bow in respect to the master of the word, to whom many owe much. We have no wreath but there is no need of one against the laurels he created for himself. I had the last word; it was solemn and beautiful in its dignity."

Blindly conciliatory pathos at the graveside. No hint of criticism or scepticism.

Master of the word. Respect. Laurels. Solemn. Dignified.

My father remained unchanged. Always the same.

*

Being gifted from the outset is an agreeable thing. Talent, in writing poems, for instance, confirms a person's individuality and makes them attractive. Extreme achievements are not required of them; it is they themselves who make or do not make such demands. For a while, it is enough simply to be gifted, the sympathy advanced them will go on increasing. It renews itself even after the second or third failure. After a few years that stage is over. Perhaps overnight, the first portentous New Year's eves arrive. Now you cannot achieve anything more with talent alone. It becomes merely the premise for a life on its own terms with no turning back. What has to follow now is the master plan. And after that come work and single-mindedness, isolation and dealing with it, despair, patience, exhaustion and daily setbacks. Sleepless toil over a sentence; renunciation of the easy way out. Scorn, disrepute, bad health and financial worries, lack of resonance or feigned interest—all in all not worth talking about any further. Writers distrust the convenience of a heroic self-profile; the romantic attitude is laughable. They are entrepreneurs among other entrepreneurs. People ask them why they do all that. Independent of support or rejection, they embody something impossible: they are living anachronisms amid the high-speed production of a limitless cultural industry. They take on their times, an undertaking without any security, and seek no justification from anyone. Whatever means life, thought and vitality now has to come forth; it forms the raw material of their alchemy. They construct a language in which everything, and nothing less than that, happens; they steel their words and set them out. They want their language to be lucid, durable and stable. The sentence they produce is everything, or they are nothing. In the structure of their world, each sentence is that stone without which it collapses. Mastery of the craft reveals itself as an illusion. Confidence in their own ability guarantees nothing. They can still founder, every day, with each word. The dubiousness of language and art, its questionable role in society, marks them for life.

Those who go on merely being talented, they fade out or go on routinely carving their groove. They can be helped; they help themselves. The structure of sentences by other people, whom they left to one side, shames their verses, but they do not know that yet. They're gifted, that means: they do not burn their tongues. They come to a comfortable arrangement with the abyss: they circle it at a suitable distance. Anarchy, protest and denial are not for them, but they value all that in others. The risk the others run cannot be great enough as far as they are concerned. They stand up, according to choice and taste, for what is right; the lifelong process of subversion remains foreign to them. They do not founder over a concept, get lost in impossibilities or perish through lack of a voice or through despair. Refuge in compromise is their legitimate career path. They have a secure place and occupy it completely. They are now available for honours and offices; they stand on secure ground and can say their piece all right. They get on by hook or by crook; all in all they get on as they should. They whistle up their words; these come to heel obediently, and do not bite but go swarming through the feuilletons. They carry on to the next verse without any risk; they have not gone beyond the pale; they know what it is to be satisfied. Their last gasp is still socially acceptable. Propaganda uses them with success. The public world seizes on them and drags them up to the cold buffet. It has an ear and microphone for them. They accept the limits it sets for them. They are its creatures.

My father had neither the chance of a public career nor the chance of an exemplary failure. For him the golden mean turned grey. He was talented, but the exercise of his talent did not make the grade. His inadequacy became a case of crushing disappointment. The last volume of poems was called DIE SCHERBENSCHWELLE (*Threshold of Shambles*). It was worse than bitter for him: he was left by the wayside.

*

His work and his thought does not contain any notions and ideas about the world or human existence that go beyond traditional concepts like homeground, fatherland, honour, wife and child and the transience of everything earthly. His views on art were classicistic and culminated in reverential formulations like DIGNITY OF THE SPIRIT and ETERNAL VALUES. Nothing much seemed to change in his bourgeois-romantic attitude, even after the end of the Third Reich. It remained a thoroughgoing German, pre-ideological domain of Blood and Soil. There are a few beautiful verses in a traditional style and individual poems whose language undoubtedly exceeds that, but poetry derived from unquestioned borrowings could not lead to any openness or to anything absolute in itself. It is the lyric poetry of a melancholic addicted to his homeground, of one who yearned for a stasis beyond the intellectual complexities of the century. It was not by chance that Adalbert Stifter was his favourite author and *Nachsommer* (*Late Summer*) his best-loved reading. My father's dilemma lay in the fact that his long obsolete notions of homeground, art and family were perverted by the Third Reich and consequently invalidated; yet he himself, returning shattered from the war and captivity, needed them more and more. Now he would have benefitted from HOMEGROUND as an unshakeable foundation in order to restore himself. It was too late; it was always too late. He was always a man who built on crumbling foundations—now the delay became a case of failure. He lived in a climate of latent tragedy, without buttresses for the ruins of his ideas, owing more and more on his losses, stumbling between melancholia and aggression. He fell silent, shrivelled, limited himself more and more. The remainder of his existence became an extended epilogue for an old world, whose ending wrecked his way of thinking and writing.

*

In literature, as everywhere, you build with bricks. Competition among the bricklayers. Great clouds of dust raised in the local and international building sites. Whilst the master mason prepares his monument without any fuss, the bricklayers show themselves off before their little sites, lay the same row all their lives and noisily offer small lengths from their fabrications.

My father was a builder of modest structures. He scorned the bricklayers and acknowledged a master mason's achievements. He was able, critically and without envy, to recognise the master masons. He took pleasure in exploring a master's edifices, the triumph of which could have shamed him. What was his small structure compared with the extraordinary constructions from a master mason. Sometimes he set one of his structures before me. I did not appreciate it; I turned my back on it. He said: PEOPLE WILL LIVE IN MY BUILDING A HUNDRED YEARS FROM

NOW! And I said: what has happened to the style, what has happened to the flair. Then he was hurt and retired behind his walls. He ranged over the edifices of a master mason and cried out: I like this place, the master mason is good. Then I shared a place with a free man. Then I loved the selfless bricklayer and thought: in this plush, prosperous moment—in this second, beyond doubt—now—and always at such times—the bricklayer shows greatness.

*

It was good to go through his countryside with him. His step was elastic and his glance up into the trees sparkled. The chronic nervous tension fell away. Such happiness as was in him then came openly into his eyes and communicated itself effortlessly. The seasons and the landscape of the Black Forest were his wealth. He delighted in the dripping dampness of the underbrush, the early mist on the mountains, the poplars in the snow. He loved the autumn; its decay refreshed him. Anything he had once noted remained familiar to him for the rest of his life. At such times you could see how much of his inner vitality had been lost. His family lived in opposition to his demands, resisted his helpless aggression. You fled the tragedies of his impoverishment and, in your aloofness from him, were not capable of recognising what had remained whole out of his dreams.

Finally there was no longer anyone close to him who could respond to the man's qualities. No one seemed to want anything from him, and what he gave away unconditionally was rejected as an imposition. His personality could not adapt easily to other people; it brooded increasingly within itself and paralysed open contacts. He did not seem to know that he was isolated. His solitariness made him blind to rejection by others.

One winter's day, we went up a valley along a Black Forest mountain stream. A hawk circled level with the mountains, drifted down and disappeared over the marsh in the valley. He watched it through his binoculars (not a step without his binoculars), lowered them and called out with intense pride: MOORHAWK, THAT'S WHAT THEY CALL HIM!

Satisfied, he went back to the car. Then ham and wine in the Angel Inn.

*

Landscape meant LANDSCAPE OF THE SOUL for him and nature was an object of constant yearning. He liked to stand on castle ruins in Baden and wish himself somewhere beyond the horizon, and he liked to stand on towers and mountains abroad and wish himself back in his own landscape. The relationship between geographical confines and expanses, between retreat into narrow bounds and experience of the wide world was emotionally fraught in him, swinging between farmhouse kitchen and cosmic PRESENTIMENT—a dilemma inherent in the German Romantic tradition. His basic instinct for nature was the good aspect. The other was the lyrical idealisation of the country and country life as an intact world. It scarcely differed from the city dweller's enthusing over nature. He loved landscape and lived in nature but knew little about the life of the farmers. When he spoke Alemannic with them, his diction was forced as he tried to make himself appear someone who belonged there. The sweating, toiling everyday life of the farmers, dominated by work, their centuries-old resignation and the hardness they gained from it, the pride, the miserliness, the stubbornness, the sharp tongue, and finally the mechanisation of agriculture—all that was remote from the aesthete's experience. He had never lived in a village. He did not know what cattle vaccination, milk prices or grain harvests were exactly. He was concerned with the cultural history of Baden (legends, customs, costume and carnival masks). The noise of a cartload of wood going down to the valley was a fine thing, but forestry and woodworking were for him, at best, something he had to imagine.

For his own purposes, he created a literary image. It was still determined by Gotthelf[4] and Hebel and maintained the notion that an archaic scheme of things was a healthy one. The relatively simple, unchanging (in the bourgeois mind grotesquely underestimated) difficulties of a farmer's life had a calming effect on a man constantly racked by new tensions. He felt good among farmers, with their ham and must, and did not seem to notice that every time they saw in him (with their sure instinct for the difference, and their pride, prudence and embarrassment) the educated man, the bourgeois, something better.

*

HOMEGROUND—that was the grease you rubbed on against the world's chill.

A comfortable, secure fortress against decay, madness, nihilism and doubt. Against the wilderness, the shivers, loss and death, dangers of all kinds and ringing in the ears. Homeground, his squid's ink cloud, the only possible security for the weakened man. That was the familiar odour that smothered all doubt. That was the self-restriction of a man to his own modest intactness and the life-long contemplation of what had been given him from birth. Homeground, the only thing with which he concerned himself. What could not be gathered onto homeground was repressed or expelled. That was the mental defence against other schemes of thought, ways of thinking and ideologies, above all against those that shifted from CONSERVATIVE to LEFT WING. HOMEGROUND, a personal kitchen where sentiments were warmed up and his feelings overcooked. Homeground. Homeground.

The chameleon sat its whole life long on the same spot because it only had one colour to call its own.

*

No-one has ever managed without the word HAPPINESS. No thinking person has ever renounced the idea of HAPPINESS. In the absence of HAPPINESS, enthusiasm for life and joy in it can be lost, but not the idea of HAPPINESS.

There are various definitions of HAPPINESS that do not mean much. HAPPINESS stands for a fortunate constellation of fate (the usual formulation) and is described as a state of soul that results from the fulfilment of wishes that are important for a particular individual. In political and philosophical systems, the hankering after HAPPINESS is affirmed as a morally justifiable motivation for human actions. In the Constitution of the United States, HAPPINESS is defined as a human right.

If asked about his idea of HAPPINESS (I did not ask him enough questions), my father would perhaps have answered: being able to move around within the scope of the landscape, being unchallenged within the family circle, work, long life and a peaceful death. Anton Chekhov would have replied: HAPPINESS was too little; it was trivial; there had to be more rational pursuits for humanity. Frank Wedekind's answer of to this question: TO BE WORN OUT AS BEFITS YOUR ABILITIES.[5]

That is a notion of happiness without illusions (no answer could be more practical). It is the sober wish of a productive personality. If this sentence can be used as a yardstick, then my father would have to count as an unhappy man (he said that he considered himself unhappy). He was worn out by a smothered childhood, by unresolved anxieties and massive repressions. He was worn out by believing in obsolete ideas and by submitting himself to their fascination. He was worn out by illusions about himself and worn out by me too, in this sense: by poems he could not possibly write.

It was not his potential but his weakness that wore him out so completely.

He was devoured by trivia.

That he should be devoured by trivia. That he should be worn out: yet not by himself.

*

The memory of an evening in May when he came back from the newspaper office, on his moped in the pouring rain.

A warmth that ran in streams; the blossom hung low in the garden; he ran into the house with his saturated briefcase. His shoes were full of water, but he laughed. A bad mood was to be expected, but he laughed; not a word about a chill. He trailed the water into all the rooms, and this time nothing worried him, neither dirt in the hall nor ruined clothes. Laughter, radiant and free, unrestrained laughter—and for me today that one burst of laughter can still reconcile me with the bankruptcy of his old age.

*

His health was failing. His hopes were exhausted.

He restricted himself to enjoying in moderation what lay to hand. The enjoyment of everyday habits in the house and the daily repetition of the familiar routine. The enjoyment of a quiet morning in his room, among books and pictures, and the enjoyment of all activities and situations that he could easily manage. Working in the garden and reading the classics. Strolling the streets that he knew from childhood. The seasons and the feast days. A glass of wine in the familiar landscape. Trips in the car to Opfingen or Sankt Märgen. The repeated creation of the same idyll. The craving for timelessness and nebulosity.

Everything else was uncertain. Everything else became increasingly burdensome and less and less certain. The world: one uncertainty too many.

THE SHREWD PEOPLE TO WHOM I DEFINITELY DO NOT BELONG.

He sought his compensation in the sound of the rain in the nut-tree outside his window.

*

He died in 1969, at the age of sixty-two.

A pension granted late in the day (incapable of work by dint of his war injury) could still benefit the sixty-year-old. He finally had no more worries, but he was used to worries and carried on worrying. He could now do what he wanted, but he did not want much. He did not wish for much more than intimacy with his family. Daily life continued more slowly with evenings in his local pub, critical pieces for the newspaper and trips into the country. He edited the works of Hebel once again, and if he did note down a line of verse occasionally, he did not type it up. Shifting sackfuls of dead leaves out of the garden, a job for October days, demanded more time and tired him. He went walking along well-known paths; the walks grew shorter and shorter and became strolls through the garden. Various illnesses aged him;—he recovered and travelled to France, seeking the LANDSCAPES OF HIS SOUL.

His will to live was unusually strong and helped him rise above the decay of his body. His lungs and his liver were damaged; his heart dangerously weakened after many attacks. Weak circulation, fever and shortness of breath, bedrest and reading in his room for weeks on end. His wife maintained the contact with the outside world. Her constant presence lengthened his life. The CHILDREN had left home years before. They made phone calls and still came to visit.

Successive therapies showed little success. Stronger dosages did not help any more. Wellbeing proved ephemeral and precious. A pacemaker was implanted in him. His body and the machine were not compatible. Treatments in the clinic could help him only as far as a conditional discharge. A sanatorium in the Black Forest did not suit him. He drowsed on towards an uncertain recovery and did not think, as far as that was possible, of death. He had thought of death all his life, but in death's front yard he did not want anything to do with it. His mouth was narrow; it became ever narrower. Energy and tension made his lips thin. His mouth flattened out at the corners and merged into one line. At the end he had no lips any more. His despair was greater than all his hopes of life, but he still made plans for journeys. He saw the snow and the blossom once again and heard the bells. He was grateful for the patience that surrounded him. In his passivity, initially enforced and then accepted, in being restricted to himself and his family, he found peace in a strange way. Self-release through suffering, that was a quiet transformation. In the excruciating, growing, unavoidable pain, in the tormented misery that gripped all his organs, in the absence of duty and of the world's affairs, he was, in a dreadful way, content. He took interest in things outside of himself, in photographs, in texts and questions about art. Interrupted by feverish sleep, he still read poems; he drowsed his way unresentfully out of his life. He died one June night in his sleep, and, as he had wished, in his own room.

His heart stopped; the pacemaker went on ticking.

Epilogue

Kannst du das Wasser verdünnen?
Keinigkeit.
Kannst du die Dunkelheit essen?
Das weißt du doch.

(Can you dilute the water?
Child's play.
Can you eat the darkness?
You know I can.)

When my father was little (that is: three years, one hundred days old), a cloud fell from the sky one morning. It fell noiselessly over the garden, grew dark and huge and made the light disappear. It slowly sank down past the trees and came to rest on its own shadow. At that point, it turned out that the cloud was a balloon.

A tethered balloon with one of those gondolas, that's right.

In the gondola stood—who was standing in the gondola? The Captain. My father was dressed in a sailor suit and wore black, polished, lace-up boots. The Captain bowed to him. My father waved back.

Let's begin, said the Captain and climbed out of the gondola. They went into the house and set to work. First, the big things and then the little ones. First, then, the tables, chairs, beds and cupboards. The Captain gave the things a tap; then the things got the message and made themselves small. The two of them carried the tapped and shrunken big things into the gondola; that makes seven times seven tables and everything else besides. Refrigerators, tiled stoves and leather armchairs. Grandfather clocks, mirrors and whatever else there was.

After that, the second-biggest things into the gondola. My father gave them a reducing tap; then they got the message and shrank down. Fry and pan, cooking and pot, cooking and stove, bath and tub. Writing and desk, nib and holder, hand and towel, pocket and torch. All that seven times over again, and who knows what as well.

The third biggest things did not need a tap. They were small; they were almost too small. They were so small that an enlarging tap would not have hurt them. So it was lids on tobacco pipes, sugar spoons and salt-cellars. Moon- and sunglasses, hay-fever horses, lighters and waterers and odds and bobs, bible quotations (ordered according to prophet), knives, forks, scissors and whatever was lying around. Rain- and sunhats and that sort of thing. Mousetraps and what belongs in them.

The fourth biggest things were the smallest and the last. They were too small for an enlarging tap. The Captain and my father knew what to do. They put on their enlarging spectacles, scrutinised the walls and the floors, peered into the air, the stillness and the light and brought the little things to the gondola. So it was mayflies, dust motes, drops of water and rays of sun, buttons from the washing, heads from the matches, ink spots and mouse-hairs. Centimetre, millimetre, bits and pieces and goodness knows what.

Then the house was still there with its rooms. The house with its roof and the roof with the tiles. The roof with every single one of its tiles. The house with the doors and windows and heaven knows what else. The paint outside and inside, the cellar floor and the earth below it. In a word: the house. It was still standing there.

They gave the house a few reducing taps—but nothing doing. The house, the house, the house did not understand them or rather: it did not seem to want to understand them. The house, or whatever it was, did not want to, and strange to say: it did not want to go into the gondola.

Then the Captain said: look here, you are the house. Take a lead from the other things. You can't shirk shrinking. Don't be like that.

The house let him talk and did not move.

At that my father and the Captain said: the others are in the gondola waiting for you. The tables, the chairs and the mirrors are waiting for you, the glasses, the forks or whatever, the keys and the keyholes and goodness knows what.

Then pleading and begging had done their bit. They had apparently talked the house round.

With a sigh it pulled in its chimney.

They gave the house a sixth and seventh tap until it was small enough for the gondola. Now the rooms were too small even for a fleck of dust; the doors still too big for nothing at all. Now the house fitted into my father's handkerchief. He packed it up and put it into the gondola.

And then?

And then the place where the house had stood was no longer covered by anything.

And then?

Then it was the garden's turn. First the beeches, the cherry trees and the elderberry. Then—singly and with great care—the bell tree, the poplarapple trees and the sunflowers. The grass, the molehills, and whatever else was there. The rowanberries and what-do-you-call-it-all.

And then?

Then it was already time for the next in line. That meant the garden fence and the mountains behind it, the woods behind it, and seven thousand people. Seven thousand for a start, but well, okay, Hinz and Kunz and Gundel Krebs, Jimmy Aschoff and Doktor Kreuder. Kürtchen and Gretel and Auntie Suzie, fat Friedrich from the Mozartstraße and Professor Ungern, who chanced to hail, all on his own, from Gürtelschnall and eated by choice nothing but red beets.

Ate, ated or eated. But well, okay.

And then?

Then it was the turn of the next-but-one things; that meant first of all a big town. For example, Paris, which stood in Denmark, not far from Hinterzarten and near Spitzbergen. Then another ten thousand people and the sparrow on the roof. The houses and railways and tramdrivers. My father—in his reducing voice—called all the things by name and blew them into the gondola. Then came the south coast of Hungary and the North Pole of Baden, the Spanish South Pole and the Tunisian Arctic. The Finnish desert and the whole of America. And about another ten thousand people, with names, but also without them, and a peace treaty. With kids and cats and cancelled identity cards. With this and that and whatever else was there.

And then?

Then came the Negroes or whoever they were. Those who had lost their colour either voluntarily or involuntarily. Those made up with shoe polish and all the others. That is, the people who live in coconuts and vote for the desert as president. The Central European street sweepers and the pretzel-eating Indians from Scotland. The Arabian researchers into Christianity and second-hand car dealers from Soiloweedia. The moorhawks, storks and plovers, the blackbirds, dolphins and foxes and some marvellous thing or other. The crocodishes and buffoonchmen, the rogues, the greenhorns and the paperboys.

And then?

They all had themselves shrunk and looked forward to the gondola.

And then?

Then came the next lot after the next-lot-but-one; what was still left, then. Flashes in the pan[1] and the freshwater sea. The Emperor of Kirchhofen, the Beggar of Tokyo, a little bit of Chicago and the woman who bakes the cakes in the Theodorstraße. All in all: the whole world and whatever else you want.

And then?

Was named and blown into the gondola.

Was named?

Was named by name and not mixed up.

And then?

Then the earth was bleak and empty, but they still stood on it. My father stood there and looked across the empty earth; the Captain stood next to him and the gondola was there.

And then?

Ah and then, oh and then.

Ah, dammitall, and oh and ah.

All well and good. But then?

The Captain and my father were still standing there.

In short: they had cleared it all away. Packed it into the gondola and goodness knows what else besides.

They could now see that there was nothing more left. The globe was round and raw, and they had nothing else to do. The gondola stood next to them and had not changed.

And then?

Blow up the balloon and godspeed! The Captain and my father blew up the balloon—and how they blew it up, each one with his own lungs. Their lungs or goodness knows what, all their puff and heaven knows what, the breath from both of them blew up the balloon.

They ate their reducing biscuits. And then? Waited for them to work and climbed tinily into the gondola. From the gondola, they gave the earth a tap with a stick. The earth—a whole globe and goodness knows what else—was very big and needed a lot of taps, did not hurry. On the contrary: it took its time. It shrank slowly under the gondola until it was small enough. My father fished the little ball out of the air and put it under the Captain's bench.

And then?

Then the balloon was the only thing far and wide. It hung in the air and did not need to rise.

Hung in the air?

Somewhere up there, down there, or next-door, somewhere buoyant and in mid-air.

Up there in the air?

It hung right up there.

And then?

The Captain and my father in the gondola. The world, or whatever that had been, in the gondola.

And then?

Light. Air. A flying gondola. And then?

Gondola.

And then?

Nothing but gondola.

Notes

I

1 Deutsche Kraftwagen-Werke: makers of a popular small car before the Second World War.

2 Adalbert Stifter (1805-1868), prose-writer.

3 In some parts of Germany, it is customary to celebrate the Saint's Day that corresponds to your own name.

4 Johann Wolfgang von Goethe (1749-1832), poet, dramatist, novelist, essayist, scientist and administrator.

5 Johann Peter Hebel (1760-1826), prose-writer.

6 A hot, southerly wind affecting Southern Germany and Austria, often unpleasantly humid.

7 The Central Uplands, stretching from the North German Plain to the Alps.

8 Wine pressed from grapes deliberately left out to be shrunken by frost.

9 Architectural term for an eight-sided Gothic tower.

10 Gottlieb Konrad Pfeffel (1736-1809), minor poet, prose-writer and dramatist.

11 The medieval town hall in Frankfurt-am-Main.

12 Ferdinand von Zeppelin (1838-1917) constructed the first German airship in 1900.

II

1 Peter Huchel (1903-1981): known above all for his poetry.
Martin Kessel (1901-1990): prose-writer.

Kurt Tucholsky (1890-1935): popular prose-writer and satirical feuilletonist.

Günther Eich (1907-1972): poet, prose-writer and dramatist.

Martin Raschke (1905-1943): prose-writer.

Horst Lange (1904-1971): poet and prose-writer.

2 Elizabeth Langgasser (1899-1950): best known for her prose-writing.

Johannes R. Becher (1891-1958): prose-writer and poet.

Bertolt Brecht (1898-1956): prose-writer and poet, but best known for his dramas.

Gottfried Benn (1886-1956): best known for his poetry.

3 Kurt Tucholsky (1890-1935): journalist and prose-writer.

4 Alfred Döblin (1878-1957): prose-writer.

Heinrich Mann (1871-1950): prose-writer.

Oskar Loerke (1884-1941): best known for his poetry.

Otto Dix (1891-1969): painter.

Oskar Schlemmer (1888-1943): painter.

Ernst Barlach (1870-1938): painter and sculptor.

5 Sturmabteilung: the Nazis' shock troops, used for violent political agitation.

6 The parliament building of the Weimar Republic between the wars; mysteriously burned down in February 1933 not long after the Nazi takeover.

7 Achim von Arnim (1781-1831): prose-writer and poet.

Bettina Brentano (1785-1859): prose-writer and poet.

8 Günther Eich: "Wiepersdorf. Die Arnimschen Gräber" in: *Gesammelte Werke* (Frankfurt-am-Main, 1973), vol. 1, p. 65.

Peter Huchel: "Wiepersdorf" in: *Gedichte* (Berlin, 1948), p.70.

9 Brecht's first play; it brought him public notice with its production in 1918.

10 Nazi slogan for a genre of agrarian Romanticism.

11 Title of a poem by Huchel: "Die zwolf Nachte" in: *Ost and West 1* (1947), 82. It refers to the twelve years of the Third Reich.

12 Nationalsozialistische Deutsche Arbeiterpartei—the "Nazis".

13 Gertrud Kolmar (1894-1943?): best known for her poetry; disappeared without trace in 1943.

14 Munkepunke, pseud. Alfred Richard Meyer (1882-1956): publisher and editor, wrote satirical poetry under his pseudonym.

Max Herrmann-Neisse (1886-1941): poet and prose-writer.

Alfred Mombert (1872-1942): best known for his poetry

15 Georg von der Vring (1889-1968): poet, prose-writer and translator.

16 From John Bunyan's *Pilgrim's Progress*: the next destination after Christian and his friends have killed Giant Despair.

17 Wilhelm Schafer (1868-1952): prose-writer.

HJ = Hitlerjugend: Nazi youth organisation.

18 Hans Carossa (1878-1956): prose-writer and poet.

19 Ernst Jünger (1895-1998): prose-writer; his *Das Wäldchen 125*, published in 1925, chronicles Jünger's experience in the trenches in 1918.

20 Hans Grimm (1875-1959): prose-writer.

Hans Johst (1890-1970): best known for his early Expressionist dramas.

Erwin Guido Kolbenheyer (1878-1962): prose-writer, dramatist and poet.

21 Wilhelm von Scholz (1874-1969): best known for his novels.

Josef Weinheber (1892-1945): best known for his poetry.

Agnes Miegel (1879-1964): prose-writer and poetess.

Karl Heinrich Waggerl (1897-1973): prose-writer.

Ernst Wiechert (1887-1950): prose-writer.

Hermann Burte (1879-1960): painter, prose-writer and poet.

22 Otto Brues (1897-1967): prose-writer, dramatist and poet.

Fritz Diettrich (1902-1964): poet and dramatist.

Adolf Georg Bartels (1862-1945): prose-writer, dramatist and essayist.

23 Georg Britting (1891-1964): prose-writer and dramatist.

Albrecht Goes (1908-2000): prose-writer and essayist.

W.E. Süskind (1901-1970): prose-writer, poet and publicist

24 From 1936 onwards, Stalin ordered "show trials" for most of the original revolutionary and military leaders in order eliminate any opposition.

Spartacus was the name adopted by a group from the Independent

Socialist Party, which became the first German communist party and staged an abortive revolution in Berlin from 5-11 January, 1919.

Walther Rathenau (1887-1922) was Foreign Minister in the Weimar Republic. He was murdered by anti semitic nationalists.

Carl von Ossietzky (1889-1938): liberal pacifist publisher, murdered by the Nazis.

25 Expressionism: name given to the new creative departures, to a great extent in deliberate opposition to 19th century tradition, in all the arts throughout Europe from approx. 1910-1925.

Dada: title given by émigré artists and writers to the aggressive, nihilistic parodies of existing art forms which they began to produce in Zurich in 1916 as a protest against the First World War.

Vladimir Majakovski (1893-1930): avant-garde, left-wing poet, influenced German writers in the 1920s.

26 Filippo Tommaso Marinetti (1876-1944): best known as the founder of the Italian Futurist movement before the First World War, dedicated to overthrowing cultural tradition in favour of an art suitable for the future age of technology.

Sergei Tretjakow (1892-1939): Director of early revolutionary theatre in the Soviet Union.

27 Josef von Eichendorff (1788-1857): best known for his poetry; this is the first verse of his poem "Sehnsucht" (Yearning).

28 Conrad Ferdinand Meyer (1825-1898): prose-writer and poet.

III

1 A further distinction awarded to the Iron Cross.

2 Lineage of the medieval Holy Roman Emperors.

3 Helmut von Moltke (1800-91): Prussian Field-Marshall and military historian.

4 Main character of the novel *The Adventures of the Good Soldier Schweyk* by the Czech writer Jaroslav Hasek (1888-1923). An anti-hero whose adventures satirise the military of the First World War.

5 Italian for maquis, Mediterranean shrubland.

6 Lieutenant.

IV

1 Joseph Christian Friedrich Hölderlin (1770-1843): poet; his novel, *Hyperion oder der Eremit in Griechenland (Hyperion or the Hermit in Greece)* was published in 1799.

2 Ludwig Christian Heinrich Hölty (1748-1776): poet.

3 Thomas Mann (1875-1955): best known for his novels; his *Der Zauberberg* (*The Magic Mountain*) was published in 1924 and is set in a sanatorium in the Swiss mountains.

4 Friedrich Schiller (1759-1805): best known for his dramas; poet and prose-writer.

Andreas Gryphius (1616-1664): poet and dramatist.

5 Hermann Kretzschmar (1844-1924): musicologist.

6 Georg Wilhelm von Leibnitz (1646-1716).

Arthur Schopenhauer (1787-1860).

Georg Wilhelm Friedrich Hegel (1770-1831).

All three men had a significant influence on the development of German philosophy.

7 Otto Eduard Leopold von Bismarck-Schönhausen (1815-1898): creator and first chancellor of the German Empire.

Peter Rosegger (1843-1918): prose-writer.

8 From the last chapter of Schweitzer's book: *Zwischen Wasser and Urwald* (*On the Edge of the Primeval Forest*) of 1921.

9 Panje is Russian for farmer.

10 Klaus Mann (1906-1949): prose-writer, son of Thomas Mann.

11 French: nothing goes any more; used in roulette to indicate that no more bets may be made.

V

1 Egon Vietta (1903-1959): essayist and critic.

Otto Bartning (1883-1959): Modernist architect.

2 In June 1948 the grossly devalued Reichsmark was replaced by the Deutschmark in the zones of occupation of the Western allies and subsequently by a similar currency in the Soviet zone. This move made saving and investment worthwhile.

3 Christian Wenzinger (1710-1797): painter and sculptor.

4 Kaspar Hauser (1812-1833): and enigmatic figure, who appeared in 1828 in Nürnberg with no traceable background and who later died of stab wounds.

5 Charles Lindbergh (1902-1974): first aviator to fly the Atlantic non-stop.

6 Denis Diderot (1713-1784): philosopher.

Giacomo Leopardi (1798-1837): best known for one novel, *The Leopard.*

The pseudonym of Henri Beyle (1783-1842): his novel *La Chartreuse de Palme* appeared in 1839.

Gustave Flaubert (1821-1881): his novel *Madame Bovary* appeared in 1857.

7 Jean-Paul Sartre (1905-1984): prose-writer, dramatist and philosopher.

Albert Camus (1913-1960): prose-writer and dramatist.

Both were central figures in the development of French existentialist philosophy after 1945.

8 Samuel Beckett (1906-1989): best known for his dramas.

Carl Orff (1895-1902): composer.

Luigi Dallapicolla (1904-1975): composer.

9 Heinrich Heine (1797-1856): best known for his poetry and satirical journalism.

Georg Herwegh (1817-1875): poet.

Gotthold Ephraim Lessing (1729-1781): best known for his dramas and for his aesthetic theory.

Pseudonym of Francois-Marie Arouet (1694-1778): prose-writer, poet, essayist and philosopher.

10 Pablo Picasso (1881-1973): possibly the most creative painter of the

20th century.

Max Beckmann (1884-1950): painter.

Alexander Camaro (1901-1992): painter.

André Masson (1896-1987): painter.

Refers to the pre-eminent role of Paris as a centre for painting in the 20th century.

11 Kurt Heynicke (1891-1985): best known for his poetry.

12 Twilight of Humanity: the most important collection of Expressionist poetry, published in 1919.

13 Franz Kafka (1883-1924): prose-writer.

Franz Werfel (1890-1945): prose-writer, poet and dramatist.

14 Refers to the superstitious belief that tears shed for the dead have to be carried around by them in a jug.

15 In Babel's collection of stories under the title *Red Cavalry* (1926), this notion appears as part of a discussion on the ethics of revolution.

16 Sozialdemokratische Partei Deutschlands: the Social Democrats.

17 Legislation added to the Basic Law of the Federal Republic to give the government in times of crisis powers beyond those granted by the constitution. Seen by many citizens as a threat to their civil liberties.

18 Heinrich Wölfflin (1864-1945): art-historian.

Arthur Kutscher (1878-1960): literary historian.

19 French: bad faith.

20 "Sie war des deutschen Pudels verfaulter Kern." Literally: "It was the German poodle's rotten core." This is a play on a famous line in Goethe's drama Faust: "Das also war des Pudels Kern!" spoken by the scholar Faust when the poodle which has followed him home turns out to be the devil, Mephistopheles.

VI

1 Arthur Rimbaud (1854-1891): poet.

2 Gerhart Hauptmann (1862-1946): best known for his dramas and novels.

Herrmann Stehr (1864-1940): prose-writer.

3 Josef Nadler (1884-1963): literary historian; he produced one of the standard histories of German literature and saw it reprinted four times between 1928 and 1961.

4 Jeremias Gotthelf (1797-1854): prose-writer.

5 Anton Chekhov (1860:1904): best known for his dramas.

Frank Wedekind (1864-1918): best known for his dramas.

Epilogue

1 The German text reads: "Das Hornberger Schießen", which is a play on the expression: "ausgehen wie das Hornberger Schießen": to come to nought. This expression derives from the town of Hornberg in which, so the story goes, either a gun-salute went off before the arrival of the dignitary to be honoured or the locals held a shooting match but forget the gunpowder.

www.ingramcontent.com/pod-product-compliance
Lightning Source LLC
Chambersburg PA
CBHW020414130626
46549CB00006B/2559